PRAISE FOR
SHADOWLINE

'He could overcome Kristallnacht, survive expulsion by the Nazis as a Mischling, endure a torpedo attack and near drowning and then expulsion to Australia on the vessel the *Dunera*. But his diary entries show how suppression of his search for love and sexual fulfilment was not so easy. The handsome Uwe Radok pursued his dangerous odyssey in Australia. This book is a new and sensitive take on the '*Dunera* boys'. But it is much more. Uwe died aged 93. He retained his diaries with their very personal memories. He put them in a tin later to be found by his daughter as he probably intended. Telling the story of deprivation and denial combined with self-doubt, the diary entries powerfully show the urgency of love, especially when faced with hostility and social denial. He could not bear to destroy his memories. His daughter elected to publish them. These two steps are heartbreaking. But ultimately reassuring for progress in the human condition. Uwe was not a "sissy". He was a hero beyond his knowing.'

The Hon. Michael Kirby AC CMG
Past Justice, High Court of Australia

'Much of Australia's history involves "boat people". Notable amongst them, the '*Dunera* boys'. I thought I knew the story well until I read the diaries of Uwe Radok. Revelatory and remarkable!'

Phillip Adams, AO, FAHA, FRSA

'It is rare to read a diary which so vividly conjures up both time and place. In *Shadowline*, Uwe Radok depicts the world he faced as a detainee in Australia during World War II and his struggles to understand and come to terms with his sexuality. It is essential reading for anyone wanting to understand the ways in which Australia experienced that part of our history.'

Professor Dennis Altman, AM

SHADOWLINE

THE DUNERA DIARIES OF UWE RADOK

EDITED BY JACQUIE HOULDEN AND SEUMAS SPARK

TRANSLATIONS BY KATE GARRETT

MONASH
UNIVERSITY
PUBLISHING

Published by Monash University Publishing
Matheson Library Annexe
40 Exhibition Walk
Monash University
Clayton, Victoria 3800, Australia
publishing.monash.edu/

Monash University Publishing: the discussion starts here

ISBN: 9781922633620 (paperback)
ISBN: 9781922633637 (pdf)
ISBN: 9781922633644 (epub)

 A catalogue record for this
book is available from the
National Library of Australia

Design by Les Thomas
Typesetting by Jo Mullins
Cover art by Les Thomas

Printed and bound in Australia by Griffin Press

CONTENTS

To Anita and Uwe,

and all refugees

EDITORS' NOTES

Uwe Radok filled twelve diaries between 1940 and 1943. Not all entries are reproduced here. For instance, we have excluded laborious notes he made on particular books, as this material adds little to our understanding. These deletions mean that the reader is required to make some jumps in time.

The entries that do remain have been edited for clarity. We edited with the aim of preserving Radok's writing style and idiosyncrasies, including the influence of his native German in sentence construction. Original spellings have been retained where the meaning is clear. Thus, Libya is rendered as Libia, and 'apologeticness', and other such interpretations, are left uncorrected. 'Na ja', which Radok used in the sense of 'oh well', was a favourite phrase, in speech and prose. We have left the phrase untranslated so as to retain the ring of the original. Radok used 'na ja' when writing in English.

While Radok's diaries are mostly in English, some entries are in German. Of the passages translated from German to English for this book, all are from the early parts of the diaries. The original diaries are in the collection of the State Library of New South Wales, Sydney.

At its heart, this book is about Radok's attraction to Fred, a fellow internee and 8th Employment Company serviceman. We are certain of Fred's identity, but have chosen not to give his German surname or the anglicised name he used after the Second World War. That would be to take a liberty, and a pointless liberty at that, for revealing his identity would not add to the book. Radok himself never used Fred's surname, and sometimes avoided his name altogether. Often Fred was simply his drug, 'the dope'.

With the exception of Fred, we have named all those of whose identity we are sure.

Jacquie Houlden and Seumas Spark

INTRODUCTION

Seumas Spark and Christina Twomey

Uwe Radok was never easily classified or quickly understood. While certain details of his *Dunera* story are unusual, it is the spirit of his history rather than the facts that mark him as different. For Radok internment was but a moment in time, a transient experience from which to learn, another step toward finding his place in the world. He approached internment as an analytical exercise, where everything was fodder for the brain. For some '*Dunera* boys' the experience of arrest and imprisonment came to define their understanding of self and determined the course of their lives. Radok was not the sort to privilege one experience above others; curiosity and an infinite capacity for introspection worked against such tidy conclusions. It follows that the *Dunera* boy label, an affectionate term applied to the *Dunera* internees and worn proudly by many, was not for him. His diary shows us why. No label could capture the complexities and fascinations of Uwe Radok.

Helmut Uwe Radok was born in Königsberg, East Prussia, on 8 February 1916, to Fritz and Gertrud (nee Vageler). Uwe was the second of their five children, four of whom were boys.[1] The wealthy Radoks led a privileged existence as members of Germany's educated class, the *Bildungsbürgertum*. Gertrud was not Jewish. Fritz was of Jewish heritage through both his paternal and maternal grandparents, though in common with many other *Bildungsbürger* the Radoks had converted to Christianity. From the time of the family's conversion in 1902, their identity was German Protestant. They were loyal Germans.

To Nazi authorities this counted for nothing. Under the Nuremberg Race Laws the Radoks were Jewish, with Uwe and his siblings deemed to be *Mischling*, first degree. In April 1938 Fritz was dismissed from his job as director of the Steinfurt railway coach factory. That year the family applied to emigrate to Australia, and in February 1939 for entry to the United States. Many Jews and others at risk of persecution had come to recognise that any home beyond Europe presented as a safe haven.

The Australian government approved the Radoks' application in August 1939, but the looming war made it too late for travel. This tragically common story had its roots in the passive and laboured response of the Western liberal democracies to the humanitarian crisis in Europe. As if to emphasise what might have been, Fritz was arrested at the start of September 1939 and placed in a Nazi concentration camp, where he would remain for three months. By this time the family had scattered. Uwe and his younger brothers, Jobst and Rainer, had left Germany for Britain, while their eldest brother Christoph was in the Luftwaffe completing his mandatory armed service.[2] Up until 1941 the Nazi Party demanded *Mischlinge* complete military service. Gundula, the youngest child, remained in the family home in Königsberg.[3] Fritz, Gertrud and Gundula would survive the war and settle in Australia in 1947. Christoph also survived. He emigrated to Australia in 1948, then to the United States in 1957, before returning to Germany in 1970.

Uwe had moved to Britain in May 1938, having earlier that year completed a degree in mechanical engineering, specialising in aircraft design, at the Technical University of Munich. For the next eighteen months he lived in Glasgow and worked as a mechanical engineer. In Britain, this twilight period between the world wars was marked by a defiant optimism as government and citizens clung desperately to the hope that another conflict might be avoided. Before illiberalism there was hope and possibility. Uwe, his brothers, Jobst and Rainer, and tens of thousands of other Germans and Austrians who had found refuge in Britain were able to live free and full lives. Uwe indulged his passion for gliding and socialised as he pleased.

New friends offered potential clues to the brothers' political leanings. At different times Ruth and Jim Pennyman of Ormesby Hall, Middlesbrough, supported Uwe, Jobst and Rainer with advice and hospitality. The Pennymans were known for championing communitarian causes, with Ruth especially

This photograph, circa 1930s or 1940s, was found in Uwe's papers. Radok family collection.

seen as political; socialist or perhaps communist. She had helped displaced foreigners before, having given succour to Spanish Civil War refugees. Thick files in the National Archives in London indicate that MI5 was watching the Radok brothers, but the British state did not interrupt their lives.[4] Or not until war came.

When Germany invaded Poland on 1 September 1939, Uwe, Jobst and Rainer decided to avail themselves of the practical and emotional support of the Pennymans and move to Ormesby Hall. They were worldly enough to know that the coming war would close quicker on them than on most. Around this time – when exactly is unclear – the British government deemed the brothers to be category A enemy aliens, which meant that they were regarded as threats to Britain. Though British authorities likely knew otherwise, they did worry that the Radoks, to borrow from wartime idiom, were not sufficiently 'pro-British'. Most other Germans and Austrians resident in Britain, rendered 'enemy aliens' by the declaration of war, would be classified C, meaning they posed no threat, or B, meaning their loyalties were unclear, and initially the British government permitted these foreigners to remain at liberty. B and C enemy aliens were not arrested until May and June 1940, after the German invasion of the Low Countries and France. Uwe, Jobst and

Rainer were less fortunate. On 24 September 1939 they were arrested at Ormesby Hall on the direction of MI5, the length of their detainment indefinite.[5]

Various possibilities may have informed the brothers' A classification. British officials tended to a dim view of enemy aliens with family members in Germany whose lives, ostensibly at least, appeared unaltered by the Nazi regime. This view darkened further if those family members were in the German military, as was Christoph. British officials had other concerns. In summer 1933, while a student at the University of Königsberg, Uwe had completed a six-week artillery course to fulfil the requirement for tertiary students to undertake labour or military service during their holidays.[6] He had sought the labour option, but his father, Fritz, had directed otherwise. Later, British officials would interpret Uwe's enrolment in the artillery course as evidence of his loyalty to Hitler's Germany. Perhaps his age, scholarly background and interest in gliding were concerns? He had the skills and resume of a spy. Nor was that all. Fritz and Gertrud had made representations on behalf of their sons to Hermann Göring, head of the Luftwaffe and Hitler's closest confidante. While Fritz and Gertrud sought only to protect their children, their naive pleas did nothing but damn them: MI5 came to know of at least one of these letters.[7] A further consideration for MI5 was that Paul Vageler, Gertrud's brother and uncle to the Radok children, was a committed Nazi.

A month before the brothers were arrested in September 1939, the Australian government had approved the Radok family's emigration to Australia. Now the brothers were threats to Britain and its allies, deemed enemy aliens of the most dangerous type. They had no fascist sympathies, but it mattered not. They were tainted by suspicion, which in wartime can be as powerful as evidence. Their A classifications would shape their lives in internment, and delay their eventual release. Rainer put it best: 'The fight with officialdom, a phantom, begins', he wrote of the brothers' arrest in September 1939.[8]

Uwe Radok, early 1930s.
Radok family collection.

After their arrest, Uwe, Jobst and Rainer spent most of the next nine months interned at Seaton, East Devon.[9] At Liverpool on the night of 30 June – 1 July 1940 they boarded the SS *Arandora Star*, which was to transport German and Italian internees to Canada. It was likely that their A classification had put them on the ill-fated voyage. In the early hours of 2 July, a U-boat torpedoed and sank the *Arandora Star* west of the Irish coast, with about 800 lives lost. Uwe, Jobst and Rainer survived the sinking, only to be marched on to another ship a week later. This was the HMT *Dunera*, which, on 10 July, left Liverpool bound for Australia. The brothers were three of about 2120 male enemy aliens on board. Most were Jews living in Britain who had been arrested and interned for no reason other than their German or Austrian nationality. These men are now known as the '*Dunera* boys'. The *Dunera* was also to transport about 410 Italian and German men with a connection to the fascist cause. Some were active servants or supporters of fascism, while others were motivated more by personal animus to Jews and liberal democrats than by a specific political ideology. Churchill's government wanted all these men, fascist or not, interned at the end of empire where they could not harm Britain.

The diary entries in this book begin with Uwe's account of his voyages on the *Arandora Star* and the *Dunera*. The power of his pen is evident immediately. His words offer fresh glimpses of the voyages and how internees wore the burdens of imprisonment and injustice. If the words *Arandora Star* now speak of tragedy, the word *Dunera* has become a synonym for suffering and cruelty. Physical conditions on the ship were dire and the internees were treated shamefully by the British soldiers responsible for their protection. Bullies and thieves among the guard detail stole what they wanted from the internees, and worse. The entries for 22 and 23 July mention internees being stabbed with bayonets, episodes about which little to nothing was known previously. Uwe's diary adds new information to the existing accounts of wanton violence inflicted by British soldiers on the *Dunera* internees.

These and other details give a sense of the psychological burden that stalked Uwe and other survivors of the *Arandora Star* sinking. About 250 German *Arandora Star* survivors embarked on the *Dunera*. Most were fascists or committed German nationalists, though about 50, including the Radok brothers, were not.[10] *Dunera* scholarship has touched only lightly on the fears of these *Arandora Star* survivors and the effect of a second perilous sea voyage in a week, the first voyage having ended in tragedy and disaster. From Uwe we get clues about this double horror. We learn also of his passage to internment at Tatura, another less familiar aspect of the *Dunera* story. While most of the *Dunera* internees disembarked at Sydney on 6 September 1940 and were then taken to Hay in the Riverina region of New South Wales, Uwe, Jobst and Rainer were among a minority of about 125 who were put ashore at Port Melbourne on 3 September and transported directly to Tatura, where they were interned, initially, in Camp 2. Their membership of this minority was decided by their A classifications and the lingering distrust of authorities.

Landfall and internment in Tatura signalled a new phase in Uwe's diary and its transformation into a remarkable document of sexual exploration. Uwe's childhood was almost exactly coincident with the Weimar Republic in Germany, a period when sexual reform movements flourished, including greater tolerance of homosexuality. His sense of entitlement to sexual experimentation may well have been common among men of his generation, but his capacity to document it so thoroughly was not. Internment diaries very rarely consider the question of sex in such depth, and are even less likely to broach same-sex desire. Uwe's willingness to do so is therefore extremely unusual and makes his diary an especially rich source for the history of sexuality in general, and internee life in particular. The conditions of internment, and the effort to seek reclassification in order to secure release, become context rather than narrative driver as his interest is consumed by the psychological drama of affairs, friendships, and a quest to understand the self.

Internment never threatened to undermine Uwe's identity as a member of the educated intellectual elite, and as a scientist. In the absence of professional challenges, he turned an analytical lens on his libido. For Uwe, this became a problem for observation, reflection and resolution. While still on board the *Dunera* he suggested facetiously that 'the best thing now would be taking Trappist vows or the like' (13 August 1940) but knew that a monk-like existence would not suit him. Sexual metaphors abound in the diary, and the one he most commonly reaches for is starvation, although at times he considers sexual attraction as an electric current that causes fluctuations in energy.

Uwe turns mostly to Freud, and to a lesser extent Marx, and sometimes even to Marcus Aurelius to understand his predicament. He concludes, after two years of internment, that the two forces that drive him are sex and work, and that these insights hold true for humankind in general. At times he wonders whether his uncertainty about his purpose and ambition, and the best career for his talents, is being exacerbated by sexual frustration. There are fevered pursuits of literature, mathematical equations, languages and various other efforts at self-improvement. And a concomitant querying of whether it is all just a way of distracting himself from more profound longings.

At Tatura, Uwe meets Fred, an architecture student. Uwe claims that a man's eyes reveal either long familiarity, willingness or at least a predilection to cross a 'shadow line'. In Uwe's conception, the shadow line seems to mark the boundary between heterosexuality and homosexuality. Freudian language peppers his attempts to understand his physical attraction to Fred. He deploys concepts of attachment, transference, neurosis, inversion, repression, the Oedipus complex and pathologies to analyse every detail of his interactions with Fred, whom he designates as 'the dope', a drug, and just once, 'His Majesty', perhaps a Freudian allusion to Fred's narcissism.

The relationship continues once Uwe and Fred leave Tatura and relocate to Melbourne, along with other internees granted permission to join an unarmed labour company of the Australian Army. They work together on labour parties and at times share a tent in camp, giving Uwe an unbridled opportunity to observe Fred at close quarters. Aside from Army work, on weekends and evenings they 'scram' away from camp, playing tennis, squash and ping-pong, and explore nearby beach, bush and parklands. In July 1942, after playing tennis and 'snoozing' with Fred in the afternoon, Uwe admits to a feeling of 'Perfect peace – if only it was permanent and post-war.'

The relative freedoms of Melbourne give Uwe the opportunity to explore and indulge in an unending round of lectures, concerts, theatre, cinema, record nights and eating out at restaurants. He meets members of Melbourne's artistic and intellectual circles, and enjoys an enriched existence while remaining cautious and judgemental about its depth and resonance with his own interests.

Uwe continues to be angst-ridden about his relationship with Fred throughout 1942, in part because the relationship is volatile, but largely because Uwe continues to think of it as a stepping-stone to a more permanent relationship with a woman. He remains ambivalent about Fred's attempts to engage women, but increasingly the diary begins to document his own dilemma of managing same-sex desire and the expectation of heterosexual marriage.

At the same time as he is studying Fred, Uwe keeps a weather eye on Anita Holper. They had met when Anita arrived at Tatura as a fifteen-year old in 1940. Anita was the daughter of Russian Jews who had emigrated first to Italy, where she was born, then to Singapore when Italy's Racial Laws institutionalised discrimination against Jews. Her brother Alessandro was a medical student, and the fascist regime barring Jews from higher education in Italy may have compounded the family's decision to leave. After Italy declared war on Britain in June 1940, the Holpers were deemed 'enemy aliens', interned, and subsequently departed Singapore on the *Queen Mary* for internment in Australia. On arrival at Tatura in September, the new internees received help with their luggage, and twenty-four-year-old Uwe first spied Anita in the kitchen. She remained in a separate compound for Italian and German families until her release in 1941.[11]

Uwe and Anita cross paths again in Melbourne in the spring of 1942 and Uwe rekindles the relationship despite some misgivings. By then Anita is working at the American Officers' Club and they begin attending plays, dances and cafes. He worries about his capacity to find sexual fulfillment in a heterosexual relationship and confesses to having barely thought about Anita for a year, such was his fixation on the vicissitudes of the relationship with Fred. His friends are not helpful, advising against pursuing Anita on the grounds that she is not his equal.

Uwe rightly detects some class prejudice in his friends' response to Anita, and is perhaps aware that her status as a refugee obfuscates a more bourgeois European background than was readily apparent in wartime Melbourne. Anita tells Uwe in September 1942 that she does not dream of marrying someone of her class; the war had robbed her of a status that her educated family had previously enjoyed.

Uwe himself never doubts his station as a member of the upper-middle-class at least. He approaches internment as an opportunity to learn how working-class people live, commenting more than once that a working-class background would be advantageous for the work he is now required to perform. By May 1942 he even allows that at times he feels 'satisfaction at a working-class existence', the sentiment itself indicating that this is a temporary rather than permanent state of affairs.

If Uwe always evinces a healthy ego, he at least tempers it with self-awareness. A scientific approach to his own psychology does not mean an absence of frustration, hurt, or, at times, bewilderment, but it does translate into an astonishing capacity to be frank about matters that others might wish away or deny. There is no discomfort about his attraction to men, a fact he treats with equanimity, although the use of euphemism at times indicates that he is aware that not everyone shares his views.

Reflecting after two years on the period covered in the diary, Uwe writes: 'The objective after all is marriage'. After all the agonised yearning for Fred and frank conversations with his friend Walter about same-sex desire, Uwe was not prepared to live a homosexual life. Uwe revealed what we would now call a queer sensibility – his interest was in sex, sexual release, and sexual fulfilment. He found this with men, but was equally prepared to explore its possibility with women.

The stereotypes that now envelop the *Dunera* boys and their place in the history of post-war Australia have conflated individual stories into an increasingly homogenous narrative, a singular triumph of good citizenship and material success.[12] Uwe Radok's diary warns us against the comforts and conceits of generalisation and mythology. He attached no great significance to his Jewish heritage, and practised none of the social, cultural or religious rites of Judaism. For a long time, British authorities suspected his loyalties, thinking he and his family may have allegiance to the enemy. He was among a small minority of *Dunera* internees never held at Hay. While imprisoned at Tatura he fell in love with a man, and met the woman who would become his wife. His arbitrary detention fostered a deep aversion to injustice, and empathy for the refugee's burden, but he cared little for the canonical doctrine that some former internees began to construct in the 1970s and 1980s around the *Dunera* story. His daughters recall a passionate, maddening, chameleon-like polymath: prickly and brilliant, preoccupied and doting, generous and difficult, a man whose zest for knowledge and experience never dimmed. The manner of his emigration to Australia made him a *Dunera* boy, but he did not choose or seek this label. In some ways Uwe Radok was the antithesis of much of what we know about the *Dunera* internees. Never does the one size tale fit all.

NOTES

1   Unless otherwise stated, the information in this introduction comes from sources held privately by the Radok family and the scholar Carol Bunyan. We thank the Radok family for sharing these sources, and Ms Bunyan for expert advice on various points of detail.

2   Rainer Radok, *Before and After the Reichskristallnacht: The History of a Königsberg Family*, chapter X, http://mpec.sc.mahidol.ac.th/radok/life/CHAP10.htm#X.

3   Peter Gillman manuscript notes for his 1980 book '*Collar the Lot!*', co-written with Leni Gillman. Notes in possession of the Radok family.

4   See The National Archives (London), PRO HO 382/543 and PRO HO 382/541.

5   National Archives of Australia (NAA), MP1103/1, E35138; NAA, MP1103/1, E35139; NAA, MP1103/1, E35140.

6   Thanks to Carol Bunyan for extended help on this point. See also Peter and Leni Gillman, '*Collar the Lot!*': *How Britain Interned and Expelled its Wartime Refugees*, (London: Quartet Books, 1980), pp. 53, 58.

7   Gillman, p. 58. The other appeal to Göring was in a letter that Gertrud Radok wrote to a school friend in 1938. The letter is with the Radok family.

8   Radok, *Before and After the Reichskristallnacht*, chapter IX, http://mpec.sc.mahidol.ac.th/radok/life/CHAP9.htm#IX.

9   Radok, *Before and After the Reichskristallnacht*, chapter XI, http://mpec.sc.mahidol.ac.th/radok/life/CHAP11.HTM#XI.

10   Thanks to Carol Bunyan for these figures.

11   NAA, MP1103/1, ZF35440.

12   Some accounts of the *Dunera* story in print and film are: Benzion Patkin, *The Dunera Internees*, (Sydney: Cassell Australia, 1979); Cyril Pearl, *The Dunera Scandal: Deported by Mistake*, (Sydney: Angus and Robertson, 1983); 'The *Dunera* Boys' telemovie directed by Ben Lewin, Jethro Films, 1985.

ARANDORA STAR, 1940

SUNDAY 30 JUNE

We depart from Seaton in the 'middle of the night'. The trip was an experience, in particular the many beautiful old trees, 'England at her best'. We arrive at Riverside Station Liverpool and board the *Arandora Star* together with 800 Italians and the first Nazis to join our transport, the conditions are partially unbearable; hot, unventilated rooms. There is absolute turmoil until 11pm when there is food and it's possible to move around a bit more. We sleep in crowded cabins but have a cold seawater shower!

MONDAY 1 JULY

We move to join the others on B-Deck where everything is working better, in particular, when it comes to getting food. There are old people and some questionable types. The ship is already travelling at full speed through the Irish Sea. Our course is zig zagging. Wales tomorrow, then not long after, the Isle of Man later to the right, to the left Ireland and to the right Scotland. The ship is definitely overcrowded, no idea about boats etc. It will take a few days for something to be organised. There are not enough life jackets. I have to make sure I get one. The sea voyage is slowly becoming almost enjoyable – as is the unexpectedly better food.

TUESDAY 2 JULY

Rainer and Jobst get up at 6 am to get bread rations; Rainer goes alone and I lie back down in shorts and a shirt. 12 minutes later there is a dull bang and shattering glass, and the sound of machines stops. The lights are not working. 'Now's the time, out!' There is smoke and gas in the hall, everyone is pushing upwards to the deck. Rainer doesn't have a life jacket either. I try to find him on D-deck, but it's not possible without light.

I see when I come back that the ship must have already sunk considerably and in particular, that most of the boats have already been released. *Titanic* scene, Italians falling into the boats, dead people between the boats and the side of the ship. The rope ladder is full of Italians, but it's still possible to get down.

In the water, it appears that the ship is still moving. The strong current makes it difficult to swim 5m forward to reach the last half-empty boat. I swim to the other side, to the next boat that is leaving and is actually already paddling away. Rainer follows; I think of using a piece of stair as a raft but then there is a disagreement in the boat about the oars and I am able to catch up; a moment later, so does Rainer. When the last boat comes past, we see that Jobst is on it; he came against the current. The ship is sinking very quickly now, it tips on end; people slide down the deck as it goes down. The deck breaks apart, far ahead, air shoots out and the ship disappears in a sea of oil. The boat returns to where the ship sank, not very efficiently despite a naval officer on the boat. We pick up many people. I am already almost completely exhausted. Dead people floating everywhere, their yellow faces are held completely above the water by the life jackets; cries for help from all sides. The boat is full, only looking for English soldiers now. We return to the other boats, where the officer takes over a half full one and goes back. A few hours are spent with a few other boats in this way and so much wreckage. Occasionally we take rafts in tow. The fear of death is dissipating, but for the moment everything is uncertain; I dread the thought of going back into the water. The exhaustion is not just physical, it's all encompassing. I see the doctor on a raft but have to leave him; I lack energy, it may mean the end.

Then a Sunderland flying boat appears – help is coming. Later a destroyer arrives, which we paddle to. Boarding is difficult, but we stay dry. People are very nice, but with indignation I know what I suspected before we were picked up is true, they would take their own people first. I look for Jobst and find a job distributing cookies; I still feel totally fine, physically. The wounded are transported at the back. The destroyer is now travelling at full speed, hopefully it will make it through at least; I dread the thought of having to go back in the water. There is hot chocolate and bread and warm food too; but space is limited. The wounded are taken to the bridge, to the doctor. A few more transports arrive in the night. Some people have died, and one is doing very poorly. There is nowhere to put him, so he has to go in the toilet. There is water for the wounded. Slowly, morning comes. I talk with the young Canadians. They are used to this, of course, and to them it is of little or no importance that we are defenceless prisoners of war. But apart from that, all the people are extraordinarily nice. Apparently, we are going to Glasgow.

SCOTLAND, 1940

Ian Brown and Uwe were close
friends. On 22 November 1939
Ian sent a character reference to
British authorities vouching for his
friend: 'until the outbreak of war
very few weeks have passed that I
didn't spend a night or a weekend
with him.'

Robert Rogerson was part of the
Scottish Gliding Union where
Uwe was a gliding instructor. On
18 March 1940 he petitioned
for the brothers' release, stating
that 'Rainer has a magnificent
physique and is extremely blonde',
and that Uwe had a 'very fine
mathematical mind'. 'If the boys
are to spend the rest of the war
years in an internment camp',
he observed, 'all I can see is the
creation of bitterness against this
country and bitterness against
Europe as a whole.'

WEDNESDAY 3 JULY

6 am. I feel very tired right before breakfast, perhaps because we are more or less safe now. When I close my eyes, I can still see, with surprising clarity, the boats far away amongst the debris, occasionally hidden by the waves.

We arrive in Greenoak and are sent below deck. Then we disembark. An unauthorised 3 cheers for the rescuers. We Germans are all together – we are apart from the Italians – in a large, draughty room with a concrete floor; we wait for a few hours for something to happen. The locals only heard we were arriving shortly before we actually did. Food arrives slowly and there is little of it. There are rumours that soon we will be moved on. But nothing happens and we have to prepare to spend the night here. I send a message to Ian, who actually appears at the window in the evening. He promises to bring all sorts of stuff – it arrives during the night, along with more from Rogerson. Everything is dead quiet, and people are sound asleep. The weaker people have been taken to hospital, and one or two follow them.

THURSDAY 4 JULY

Our wait continues and clothing is distributed, incomplete odds and ends. We read the newspaper reports. Ian is back again. The UK is all set for an invasion and they view these things as the inanities that they would be, if I had not spent the last 3/4 of a year as an internee and gained a bit of perspective. In the evening I have a long talk with Ian and even more supplies arrive. The children and working-class people of Greenoak are kind. Without them, things would be much worse as far as food and cigarettes are concerned. The organisation is very poor and the treatment would be called brutal if it were intentional.

FRIDAY 5 JULY

In the morning Ian comes, this time I even get to see him. In the afternoon we are taken to Edinburgh. There are no guards in the cabin, this level of trust is shocking. It's a nice ride from Greenoak to Glasgow, afterwards we drift off to sleep. The bus takes us to a camp, where it looks like the Italians had been before us. We are put with the Nazis again, but after some effort, they separate us, as much as is possible. The treatment is rough and not very friendly at first. At night a lot of people try to 'run', and that makes the guards fire their weapons. Since we've been gone from Seaton, things are really starting to look like war and now things are completely different in the newspapers and in terms of public sentiment. They are all fully prepared in any case, and it becomes a home affair.

SATURDAY 6 JULY

We are trying to get used to the new camp; the organisation is still bad; it is that way everywhere in this regard and the earlier we get used to expecting nothing – at least until we reach Canada – the better.

We complete registration; hang around and have nothing better to do except relive what we've been through.

SUNDAY 7 JULY

The weather is still stormy. There are toothbrushes and combs, still no cigarettes or chocolate, but there is an inspection. Everyone is feeling mutinous and is in quite a bad mood. So, the rumour on the destroyer that people in London were getting worked up about treating refugees in this way had nothing to it after all – I don't blame them. In Seaton, we just didn't notice the change that has happened everywhere.

MONDAY 8 JULY

I spend the whole day lying in the sun. There is not much food and one dreams of the days when things were different. Thinking about our situation in general, it's damn hopeless regardless of what happens to us. If there is no peace this year, then this idleness could last a lot longer. Maybe we really ought to try our hand at seeking donations if we really do get to Canada. But will we make it there, or will we go to Wales for the rest of the war? I occupy myself with methods, integral factors and theories of addition using Euler's formula.

TUESDAY 9 JULY

Cold and windy. Apart from that, everything is the same. Feeling hungry and unsettled; the main thing, though, is the lack of any immediate purpose in life, the existence of which would make everything else unimportant. If only it were possible to conduct a scientific experiment. Memories in the evening and a serious money problem. If the people here were a bit more reasonable and did not essentially put us on the same level as the Nazis, it would be easy to be consistent and to forgo money and passports.

DUNERA, 1940

WEDNESDAY 10 JULY

Our departure is accompanied by an uncomfortable escort. But given the current situation it's understandable that nerves are on edge. Bus ride to Liverpool, where we wait for many hours, first in the train, then by the ship. Apparently, we are going to be joined by many of the Isle of Man internees. There are piles of luggage on deck. The ship makes a good impression, which ends in a mass of barbed wire on deck. I end up on the lowest deck, nothing for sleeping on or anything, just the bare floor. Until recently this would have been met with significant protest. Our cigarettes and luggage are taken away. Summary of the day: being given the newspaper is the only glimmer of hope.

THURSDAY 11 JULY

Settling in and getting organised happens more quickly this time, the deck is off to a good start. It won't be possible to get out in emergencies, only via the shafts. The guards are very strange; they view our luggage as their property and even take away watches and fountain pens. One is a bit higher in rank and has beer bottles with 2 open. A bit reminiscent of what it must have been like in 1918. However, there is no general drunkenness. Maybe we shipwreck survivors are in their bad books thanks to the newspaper reports and they are looking for a reason to shoot. Or maybe a hand grenade will come through the shaft. Also, there is the constant fear that 'the' bang will come at any moment and will be better this time, because we are at the back. In principle, no one would come after us. Quite unsettling for a while, then suddenly everything loses its meaning; one cannot do anything more than die. A strange sense of calm at this thought alone.

FRIDAY 12 JULY

Very restless night. In a semi-awake state, I see a constant vision of the explosion and the panic that began afterwards, trembling like an animal. But the evening and morning become the following day. We are travelling at a reasonable pace and the environment changes accordingly, lying down is most comfortable. In spite of the washing and cleaning of the Augean stable, there are no difficulties. At dawn, the vision of before appears over and over: sometime in the next few minutes, it will be time. Every bang or loud breaker makes me jump. Twice, panic breaks out. Blocked exits and shots fired by the guards because the second door, which was stupidly nailed shut, broke open. Security is organised by Nazis, but they behave rationally. Still, it is easier to sleep when you know other people are keeping watch. Rough seas in the evening – good if there are U-boats, bad if – but best to leave the second part unsaid. We seem to be travelling north the whole time. I'm awake from 2–4 in the morning.

SATURDAY 13 JULY

Jobst's *birthday*. It ought to be a good omen. 4 am: destroyer and other ship are off; hope that goes well. Calm sea, the mood has improved in general; panic subsided, largely due to the calm weather. The course is strange – we cannot tell where we are heading. I walk on deck in the late morning – have already grown weak in the knees. I temporarily forget our surroundings – once remembered, they seem particularly intense and terrifying. If another attack were to happen, I would have survived the majority

Jobst turned 23.

8

of events already. Every loud noise makes me jump. Evening on deck enjoying the sun, even if it is from behind barbed wire; I notice this insignificance and relax. Wash and shower in the evening; there are the regular jumps and starts as I fall asleep and it is difficult to relax.

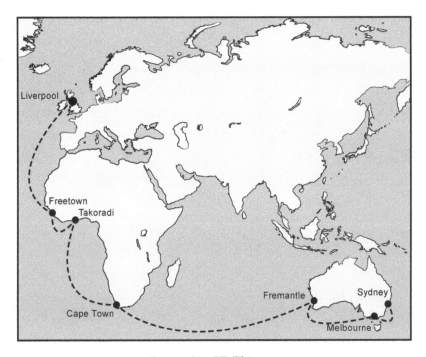

Voyage of the HMT *Dunera*
The *Dunera* departed Liverpool on 10 July 1940. It arrived at Freetown on 24 July, and departed the same day. The next stop was Takoradi, where the ship anchored from 27–29 July. On 9 August the *Dunera* left Cape Town, having arrived the previous day. The ship arrived at Fremantle on 27 August, where it stayed for one day, before heading east for Melbourne, which it reached on 3 September. On 4 September the *Dunera* left Melbourne for Sydney, where it arrived on 6 September.
Adapted from a map created by Kara Rasmanis, and reproduced with permission.

SUNDAY 14 JULY

Much the same; I grow used to the rocking of the ship and, in part, to the conditions as well. But on occasion, there is a sudden awareness – maybe quite a good thing, because an attack can always happen. It is easier for those who are less 'crazy'. For the first time <u>having</u> to think is a disadvantage. Our suitcases have disappeared into the hatch – na ja, they can be the tribute.

MONDAY 15 JULY

Calm day; tension decreasing in spite of occasional attempts to point out that really, everything is still in limbo. It is getting warm. In the morning and evening, I do washhouse duty with dirty work and repairs. Late in the evening, washing day with all the Italians. Thinking about the future is perhaps the best thing to do to combat danger. Everything seems to be so dreary, in particular, if the war goes on. I'm fed up with being a prisoner. We have to get used to 'being at war' – if we want to make it out of here. Rumours of plundering.

TUESDAY 16 JULY

Point duty in the morning; I will have to organise it myself. Short walk in the afternoon. We are heading south! Perhaps Australia after all? It would be bad – the heat under these conditions and the length of the journey. The sea is indescribably blue, the sun is very high. If it's Canada, we should see land the day after tomorrow – or at least be close to it. In the afternoon, our valuables are taken as well as razors, etc. Will we see them again? We are slowly beginning to understand the assurances made by British officers. The systematic degradation is brutal and disgraceful. They've stopped short of confiscating our toothbrushes.

WEDNESDAY 17 JULY

Dull day. The guard says of his own accord that we are going to Australia. It cannot be ruled out. But it could also be a rumour. In the afternoon, the sun is on the deck. First cigarette in a week. Very nice. I talk to a reasonable guard in the evening – being able to share my thoughts and only rarely being met with objection – like someone from Conrad. I must learn to listen. Still mostly heading to the south.

THURSDAY 18 JULY

We would have to turn west soon if we are heading to Canada. Nice weather. I get a book by Conrad; fantastic. There is a guard rotation after four days – I'm just not suitable as an organiser. Cigarettes really throw one out of tune; they are very nice at the start, the flavour is good throughout, but the after-effects aren't nice. The rumours that we are going to Australia intensify. Our surroundings slowly begin to jar the nerves – things will certainly become significantly more trying. I must really become quite desensitised – the mess in the lavatories is enough to leave one cold. The terror has faded entirely, apart from some very occasional memories. I begin to be surprised at myself. Interestingly, I had two similar thoughts in recent days – in these sorts of situations, my imagination ends up causing more trouble. In the evening, there is a gloomy, cloudy atmosphere over the ocean – it would be quite wonderful paired with the comforts of the guard detail and their freedom – and even they do not have much.

FRIDAY 19 JULY

Further indications that the journey will be long. The weather changes to cloudy. Apart from that, I spend a tired day – perhaps due to constant diarrhoea, my outlook on life is pessimistic. I make a futile attempt to brush up on spherical geometry in order to measure latitude. My temper is wearing thin; I often catch myself with clenched fists and set teeth.

SATURDAY 20 JULY

Long walk, very nice; I have grown unbelievably weak already. The barbed wire has finally been expanded a bit. In the afternoon 'definite' news that it is Australia. There is also news about a German raider in the Atlantic. It's fate – though, so much bad luck at once would be strange. If only we had no one else to worry about – and we are more and more getting used to that thought. According to calculations we must already be on the same latitude as Bermuda. Good fun, that.

SUNDAY 21 JULY

I take a long walk, the sun is very high, almost 1 o'clock. I have a peaceful talk with Africans; they are generally a good source of information and tell us that by Wednesday, we will be in Freetown, 10 degrees north of the equator. Then 10 days on to Cape Town, 14 to Fremantle and a few more to Sydney. It's a nice prospect given these conditions. Maybe we will get our luggage back after all, or otherwise we can make ourselves light clothing. Anyway – it's fate and we can't do anything about it. I go to the doctor for diarrhoea because of the possibility that it might be the start of something. I went back to fetch my kit and could not get back to the hospital. It's fine since I feel all right – apart from feeling slightly weak in the knees.

MONDAY 22 JULY

Very warm. I spent yesterday doing spherical geometry. Miscalculated today and tried again. There is a sudden crackdown in the afternoon. Everyone on deck. The usual search upon our return. One man is stabbed with a bayonet, but certainly at least it was partially his own fault. Wedding rings, fountain pens, all our chocolate gone. Glorious day for the British Army. But upon cooler reflection this is still one of the milder of wartime fates. In terms of the soldiers, it is like in Kipling – also paired with some criminal tendencies, which some of these people definitely display. Recently I've talked to S in the evenings – the best and only attitude is to be completely passive. We have nothing left to lose, if we really do make it to Sydney – I should consider myself lucky – we might even be released and otherwise it's all the same. I couldn't really muster up much sympathy for this lot either. It's my bad luck to be one of them for the moment; but hopefully it is not forever, though that is possible. I saw lots of flying fish and dolphins yesterday. The colour of the bridge has changed from camouflage to brown. There are rumours of peace.

TUESDAY 23 JULY

In the night, someone was stabbed in the stomach by a guard with a bayonet. Fortunately, he is not dead. The soldier may have fallen asleep and gotten scared, thanks to the stupid rabble rousing, which is primarily at fault. In the late morning, a new swathe of barbed wire is opened; lots of noise and jostling, but for the moment there is little improvement to see. Nice sunset in the evening, and high clouds that reflect on the water – flaming bronze. Jobst puts an end to my venting in the morning – really, he is right; I should keep a handle on my antipathies here. He only does so at the table and through a healthy dose of egoism manages to keep that tension rising at a slow rate. Based on time, calculations show we are on the latitude of Freetown now.

WEDNESDAY 24 JULY

In the morning, there is land in sight and other ships, in the east. Mountains. We anchor in Freetown in the late morning alongside aircraft carriers and other ships. The mountains are reminiscent of Scotland, but the air is very clear, individual palm trees are visible and there are silhouettes of dugout canoes. Long, stretched out flat coast, very African. Later, there is a tanker alongside us. We cannot get any water here, so fresh water is rationed and not allowed for washing and that's without having changed clothes at all. I try to make shorts from a straw sack, and make thread. Fight with the needle – no real reason, but certainly mutual. In the evening, we are back at sea. All of Sierra Leone is visible in the twilight, even individual lights. There is a brightly lit Japanese ship in front of us. Rumours that peace talks are underway.

THURSDAY 25 JULY

High seas. I'm feeling rather unsettled but decide no walk, it is too unpleasant and dangerous because my response of 'fucking bastard', the suitable response to 'British hero', could and would lead to useless unpleasantries. I dreamt of quite typical pre-war freedoms – we sometimes live more for the nights than the days now. This is all absolutely ridiculous and when will it be normal again? I started making the pants.

FRIDAY 26 JULY

I finished the pants and now have no immediate goal, which means once again being confronted with thinking of the real world and the future.

SATURDAY 27 JULY

The clouds look like land – in a few hours we get to Takoradi, Gold Coast. Apparently a very unpleasant place in summer – now it is cool, though dusty. A nice group of palms. We load up on fresh water again and will stay until Monday.

SUNDAY 28 JULY

Still in Takoradi. I read Russian poems. Spend time on the calculations in the area of conformal mapping – all very elementary, the only thing 'one' can do without any tools, unfortunately. The thing to do would be to write a story with no war or anything unpleasant. Sometimes I feel close to doing so.

MONDAY 29 JULY

We leave Takoradi early in the morning. Fog and rain. After yesterday's hysterical jolliness, there is already general irritability at breakfast. There appear to be two general methods: constantly neutralising my irritability in short bursts or suppressing it entirely for a while – managed carefully by the ego – and then letting it all out in one big explosion. There is the danger that I will lose sight of the bigger picture and then after successfully suppressing it, letting it all out doesn't help anymore. There are rumours that we will be released soon – but these have been incorrect many times before. I heard guards speaking as if the war is already over. Night the way it always is after leaving port. I dream of soap, that's how far it's come.

TUESDAY 30 JULY

One guard is unusually friendly, maybe there is something to the rumours after all? If there really were peace, like the Spanish refugees, we would be kept behind barbed wire because there is hardly a country that would want us. A year ago, I was flying a glider in Feal in Scotland.

WEDNESDAY 31 JULY

It is getting a bit rougher. A vision of catastrophe is hauntingly strong again – for no real reason. Even though the cage does present a particular problem, if something were to happen, we are all pretty much in the same boat. The fact that there would then be no continuation of life is decidedly uncomfortable; I can imagine it very easily and apart from this thought and the first moment one realises one is for it, there is little to it. No real desire to do anything; I'm on washroom duty.

THURSDAY 1 AUGUST

More wind and ocean. Freshwater day, laundry. I want to do some maths in the evening – cubic equations – because there is not enough room on deck. The guards seem to be getting used to things; one uses his keys and together with the internees beats out march music; the other is talking about the news that a German raider hit an English warship yesterday and the raider left damaged. However, the next guard is very nervous – there was almost an accident when a boy tried a 'trick' with a box of matches. There are rumours that some of the prisoners will be set free in Australia – it might mean the end of the war, or just reasonable treatment of the refugee issue – not bloody likely.

FRIDAY 2 AUGUST

There is a feeling of not being able to imagine being 30 or older. Of course, we can't assume anything, it's nothing of our doing whether the thing will happen or not, so it's unreasonable to worry. There is a change of weather in the afternoon, more subtropical clouds, rain squalls. Calculate at sunset, 10* east and 12–15* south; that would mean Cape Town mid next week.

SATURDAY 3 AUGUST

In the morning, I feel in the grip of terror as of old; then suddenly I remember a Shakespeare quote from Julius Caesar

The coward dies a thousand deaths
The brave but one

And strangely that 'helped', like the adage of a prayer wheel. I watched the sunrise in this way, complete with dawn colours and clouds lit up red from below. That brings the calculation to 10* E, 11* S, which is more likely than yesterday's figures. Lots of swallows, and albatrosses as well. Lovely dawn colours.

SUNDAY 4 AUGUST

Sunday with all the harassment on deck in the late morning. Like Stevenson's *St Ives*, started with a complaint about the impossible British authorities, who only allow two shaves a week. Then our colonel responded: 'you'll have to grow a beard', because apparently internees are forbidden from having razors. There has been no significant progress in 100 years. Saw albatrosses, mostly in the evening. They fly in rather short beats, a fine sight. From the front they look like a super modern plane. Every day, we're surprised that we're still here – the same for three more days, then we will be in Cape Town.

Lieutenant Colonel William Scott commanded the British soldiers assigned to guard the *Dunera* internees. He was not sympathetic to the internees and their plight, and his men abused internees with impunity. In 1941 the British Army reprimanded Scott for the manner in which he discharged his command on the *Dunera*.

TUESDAY 6 AUGUST

High waves and wonderful sun. Albatrosses fly past every half hour. I sew a collar. Sunset first, then we will be in Cape Town.

WEDNESDAY 7 AUGUST

In the morning it seems we have gone in a circle. Seagulls. Looks like land. The ocean is very calm once more. Nice sunset in the evening and after that, visible beacons on land.

THURSDAY 8 AUGUST

In the morning, the lights from Cape Town appear, then the city itself. Lovely location, modern buildings that climb the sides of the mountain. Fog blankets the mountain and the surrounding peaks. Rumours that some of us would be unloaded here so far appear unfounded. On these sorts of occasions, I am particularly aware of the fact that I am locked up – but the journey is half over now. Significant irritability – but it will get worse. In the evening Cape Town is peacefully lit up, very beautiful. P, another internee. It often takes a long time to notice someone like this, but it is nice that everywhere, even here, you meet people who are worth it.

FRIDAY 9 AUGUST

Clear and cold. We get a good view of Cape Town and Table Mountain and the inland mountain range. We depart in the evening. It is devilishly cold, but the view of the city under the cliffs at dusk is wonderful. This is somewhere worth coming back to. A big swell further out makes the ship rock. The night is typical of one after a departure though actually there is not much fuss. Are we getting used to things? There is some irritability during the day – my theories about the aggressive outbursts are confirmed.

SATURDAY 10 AUGUST

We are heading east against the huge swell; the wind is against us.
Albatrosses are already floating on the waves. The entire flock usually
sails along in front of the waves, and it looks like they are riding it. Some
fly over the water. They land elegantly in the water without flapping
their wings, and coast for 1 metre. When gliding, their wings, as they
rise, bend up. They are still there by the light of the moon. Heading east
now; Africa disappeared from view this morning. I read a newspaper
from the 9th of August. Now that Italians are in Norway, an attack on
England is expected in 1–2 weeks. There is French-Japan tension in
Indochina – just what we needed. Apart from that, only battles in Africa.
A steamship that was travelling here has gone missing – probably a
surface raider. I wonder if we'll ever get to Australia.

SUNDAY 11 AUGUST

The swell has changed, now it's going the opposite way, almost no wind,
but enough for the albatrosses, which fly very close to the sunny side this
time. They steer by twisting their wings individually or together? They
have 2 joints in the wing. Their tail is rarely used. Very aerodynamic.
Very good. General irritability is growing – as is mine. I must take more
care. Very warm again.

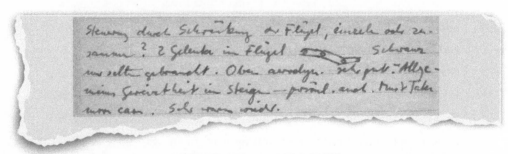

MONDAY 12 AUGUST

Fog on the surface of the water – it looks like sudden cooling, perhaps
icebergs? The wind is a bit stronger and albatrosses are more at their
ease; strong diagonal steering movements, frequently working as a

team so that the wings bounce over every little wave. I finally do some calculations, but these are incorrect (logarithmic spiral on a globe). Afterwards, I feel fed up and exhausted and have no desire to do anything. If only I knew more music or poems by heart.

TUESDAY 13 AUGUST

The surroundings have changed a lot, cloudy, cumuliform clouds and cooler during the day. We must have been in a warm current and left it yesterday. The albatrosses are almost completely gone – which would indicate we are further north. The general irritability continues to grow – but the prospect of a fistfight loses a lot of its darkness when one is irritable. The best thing right now would be taking Trappist vows or the like; one must try it, but it takes some getting used to. All that occupies one's dreams now is the current situation; everything else has left the subconscious entirely. We heard a rumour that another ship carrying 9000 men was torpedoed and sank – at least we have learned how little we know about everything and that it will take years of work and everything to focus on individual things.

Few aspects of the *Dunera* story have attracted as much conjecture and myth as the torpedo incident. On 12 July, U-boat U-56 fired two torpedoes at the *Dunera*. Neither found its mark, though one may have grazed the ship's hull on its way through the water. The few known facts about the incident are now presented in various versions, with different additions and levels of emphasis. Some *Dunera* men heard a torpedo scrape past, others the 'muffled bangs' of torpedoes exploding under water. A few attested to feeling the ship move when a torpedo touched the hull. A further account, made popular decades after the war, has it that the U-boat captain spared the *Dunera* after he discovered that Germans were aboard. That tale originated in a novel and owes nothing to fact.

WEDNESDAY 14 AUGUST

Cold. Slowly one begins to believe that it's possible we might arrive soon. In the afternoon, lots of albatrosses.

THURSDAY 15 AUGUST

Fewer Albatrosses. Astonishing story of a dent in the side of our ship from an undetonated torpedo on day 1. Not impossible.

FRIDAY 16 AUGUST

Beautiful clouds with sharply distinguished crests. After that, there are lots of clouds from the direction of the big swell, which has almost passed now. There are complaints about how we will likely be treated by the Australians – will certainly be anything but pleasant. But in the long run…

SATURDAY 17 AUGUST

More wind and ocean. Beautiful albatrosses in flight. I play a lot of Bridge – but it is a difficult game if you are not that interested in it.

SUNDAY 18 AUGUST

More wind and ocean. The weather we really should have already been having. The boat is heavy and seems to be top-heavy – which brings to mind metacentric height. In this ocean it would be difficult to release lifeboats. The fact remains, if something were to happen, then it would be over for the majority of us. Lovely albatrosses in flight – in this weather, they're really showing what they're capable of. I play Poker in the evening – that is the card game. It goes quickly and has few rules and like Bridge, it requires psychology. I forget everything for a few hours. In the evening, I have unpleasant memories of Seaton due to rations being delayed – sometimes it would be good to be a prize boxer. The boat moves a lot in the night. 3:30am the machines stop for some reason. But I have become used to scanning for danger and work out that everything is o.k. on deck. The ship is unusually quiet, sways a lot, but everything is actually o.k. and 2 hours later, we continue.

MONDAY 19 AUGUST

During the day there is a strong wind, and the ocean is very high in the evening, short and angular. But with the necessary exhaustion. I occasionally feel full of beans of some kind but under these conditions, it is very difficult to make something of it. There are rumours that the journey will end next Saturday in Fremantle. Qui vivra. According to the most recent news, England is about to be invaded; it is unimaginable, and I shudder when the subject comes up.

TUESDAY 20 AUGUST

We passed over a particularly tall breaker last night and a stack of cutlery went flying. This is a sinister indication of what would happen in an emergency. But as soon as I am awake, I am able to process these false alarms in peace. Wind is gentler during the day, heading east; it must be a low passing us, heading from SW to NE. Southern hemisphere weather – old dreams once again have meaning and set the scene for a day – together with a good book, at least as far as flying is concerned – *Night Flight* by St. Exupery.

WEDNESDAY 21 AUGUST

Wind SW again, clouds disappearing, but there are a few rain showers. A new low? During our walk a man goes overboard. His South American visa was destroyed when everything was plundered. It really makes me aware of the cruelty of it all. Thousands of people given refuge, with the knowledge that almost none of them could be saved if something were to happen. Let's hope not. Progress slows in the evening, perhaps we have already gone too far.

On 21 August, Jakob Weiss jumped overboard into the Indian Ocean. Weiss was an Austrian Jew, 36 years old. His suicide is thought to have been prompted by the despair he felt at not being able to emigrate to Argentina. This possibility, already made unlikely by his circumstances, had been extinguished when British guards on the *Dunera* wilfully destroyed his emigration papers.

THURSDAY 22 AUGUST

Wind NW – SW, is it a new low? Little sea so far, small, short waves in the dark. Refreshing in the evening and rain. Horrible increase in speed, I spend a restless night.

FRIDAY 23 AUGUST

A west wind is more intense. It is very refreshing during the day, and quite reasonable in the evening. The way the ship moves is decidedly unpleasant, but so long as I don't complain about it unnecessarily, I quickly get used to not expecting the worst every time we go over a crest. Still another 3 days to Fremantle. According to a radio message from Australia, a large number of the internees are meant to be released. Chances are not too bad, then.

SUNDAY 25 AUGUST

Wind and waves as before; based on my calculations, we are almost there. The news mentions 3 air raids on London, 'some damage'. So, in comparison, it wouldn't be very important if we popped off here.

MONDAY 26 AUGUST

Calm ocean, and now waiting to see land. In the evening, we are told that contrary to the promises made by 2 officers, we will not receive our valuables until after we land. Unofficially, we hear that they were thrown into a big heap and therefore have practically been given up. There are no words for this cruelty, even though we should be used to it by now.

TUESDAY 27 AUGUST

In the morning, land, an island, a cliff, and behind that Fremantle, Australia. It looks good. All sorts of trees, sun. Later, we are at the quay. Bustling streets, it's an unbelievable evening, everything is lit up peacefully. We are definitely not being unloaded here, it's Melbourne or Sydney. First impression is a split between pros and cons.

WEDNESDAY 28 AUGUST

We depart Fremantle at 8:00 in the morning – all as usual. Based on the newspapers, it seems like the war will last a few years. A lot of noise in the night, everywhere more or less; bad stomach ache.

THURSDAY 29 AUGUST

It is as if I had never set foot on land. The same old swell from the SW, etc. E. detained because of supposedly protesting about the food, which was bad form. Fishy, since the deck leaders participated and there did not appear to be talk of bad form for them. It probably does have to do with our valuables. In a few days, everything will be forgotten when we can tolerate it. In the afternoon, there is a refreshing wind, very large albatrosses. That will be the one lasting impression of this – an albatross in the curve of a wave against the evening sky – black and white feathers along the knife-shaped wings.

'E' may have been Dr Franz Eichenberg (1899–1981), a company director from Hamburg. Eichenberg was active in speaking for internee concerns, both on the *Dunera* and later at Tatura.

FRIDAY 30 AUGUST

Bridge and feeling fed up. Completed calculations of the logarithmic spiral on the globe. Good pace in the afternoon.

SATURDAY 31 AUGUST

We complete registration for disembarking in Melbourne together with the Italians, Nazis and the others who attracted unpleasant attention on this journey. Finally solving this problem in style after all the many promises. Two days beforehand there was an exact list with statements about the classifications for each individual – and here is the result. The worst part is that it worsens our prospects of being freed – otherwise it would not matter so much. The strange information we were given, 'wait a few months and maybe' makes sense now. But it makes little sense to fight that; the most important thing now is reaching land, which is not actually guaranteed. Tomorrow I have cooking duties for the last time. The tension already appears to be decreasing somewhat and this disappointment has me feeling fed up.

When the *Dunera* reached Fremantle, Captain A. R. Heighway, Australian Army, boarded the *Dunera* for its journey to the Australian east coast. A diligent and conscientious officer, he was responsible for documenting the arrival of the internees. He would have been involved in selecting which internees would disembark at Melbourne.

SUNDAY 1 SEPTEMBER

It is one year since my last Friday in Glasgow. We are making good progress and hopefully tomorrow evening we will be close enough to see land and when this is over, it will be enough to outweigh the other disappointments. After all what does it matter. There is a convoy with four large ships. In the evening, I read *Kai Lung*, based on my calculations, we are already quite far and should see land by Monday evening.

MONDAY 2 SEPTEMBER

Strong South wind and the albatrosses are fantastic. They start off moving through water (typical duck feet), then 1–2 small beats and then a powerful racing start in the ship's updraft. We are meant to be unloaded tomorrow and that is still the same. There are grim prospects but it makes no sense to worry too much, it will certainly go wrong. The Australians are bound to behave shabbily.

MELBOURNE
TO TATURA, 1940

In the morning, we see Melbourne bay, it is as smooth as glass. We arrive in Melbourne around 9 and are then unloaded directly into the train. Exit *Dunera*, there is some luck after all. In the train, there are very nice, older guards. We depart shortly after and travel through Melbourne via Donnybrook and Seymour to Tatura. En route, we are unexpectedly given lunch. I am no longer used to that and missed this sort of perhaps unintentional friendliness a lot. A lot of wooden houses and flowering fruit trees. Otherwise, it is flat and wide empty, it is the way one imagines Australia to look. From Rutherglen station we are taken by bus to the camp, corrugated iron huts on a mount. Italians on the right, we are on the left, with barbed wire in between. Everything is very new and solid, but this sort of camp looks a bit depressing at first. At night, it's rather cold, with a beautiful starry sky, there will be plenty of opportunities to look at it here. Apparently, getting out won't be possible for the time being. Still, we have the 'nourishing' earth beneath us again now and can slowly begin to learn that not every bang is a torpedo.

A few days later and things in the camp are settling down. The people are extremely nice and very different to what we expected. The food is good, but there is not much, that will probably change. Hopefully we will be able to get books soon and pass the time in a useful way and then we can wait to see what happens. At least the sleeping arrangements simulate some sort of privacy. During the day, you can go to an empty hut. No news or anything else of course, but you get the feeling that the people here are doing everything they can. Either the war will end this winter or England will have to fight for some time and then we will be freed. If it doesn't happen earlier, we can help out by firefighting in the north, where they don't have enough people. But it will be at least 6–12 months.

After ~ 1 week: Food is still scarce but very good; it has become one of the day's 'fleeting joys'. I started a math course. Camp life is peaceful so far but long-term there will be trouble. But compared to the last 2 months it's not bad. Our prospects for getting out aren't looking too bad. We just have to wait a bit. In my experience, that waiting ends all of a sudden. Australia is still very nice.

Will be true for quite a while.

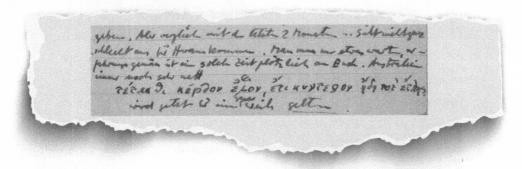

TATURA, 1940

MONDAY 18 NOVEMBER

It's miserable to be stuck here, I'm feeling a bit lost. Occasionally I become a bit stale. We don't live here, it's a fool's existence in a world gone mad. The proof is in the newspapers where they are starting to write about Huns again. But it's no use thinking about it.

WEDNESDAY 20 NOVEMBER

After a 'world' overview philosophy lecture which was quite good, considering the audience but otherwise not very surprising, I have a discussion with Fred. Author, translator; passionate, Austrian and anti German. He finds, perhaps because we grew up superficially out of necessity, modern youth are too cold and without idealism or belief in good and justice. There was more distraction, more to deal with in terms of what was going on and new achievements. Because of that, other things like art and poetry were neglected. Look at the world from the other side, it's only natural, as the neglect of art and poetry probably brought about this disaster. How naive everyone is not to see it.

The Fred mentioned here was probably Richard Flatter (1891–1960), an Austrian lawyer, author, and translator of Shakespeare.

FRIDAY 22 NOVEMBER

My train of thought stops, it opens up certain insights into long-held problems – why I am that way. It was a mistake to go straight from high school to university and it was difficult to get through it. Going with the flow probably made more sense up until now. But who knew? In any case, it suddenly seems good to be here and not sleeping in an underground station or having to bomb the Allies. If I can so easily lose my 'subject' and overview, how much easier is it then? I can't go on fooling around everywhere after all. It's a great opportunity for analysis and fixing up something.

THURSDAY 28 NOVEMBER

I attend a lecture on analytical psychology and dream evaluation. For Jung, dream has a meaning or purpose, versus Freud where it has a reason.

MONDAY 16 DECEMBER

There is good news from Europe, the first 'political' news we have had.

TATURA, 1941

Everywhere I look I come across gaps in my skills and it becomes a serious problem. Everything here indicates fragmentation, a direction is not easily discovered. On top of that, it could be very much the wrong direction, but what is the right one? Perhaps that could be determined by analysing the times when I was satisfied; but that is not very confidence-inspiring, because there are too many factors involved that should not be taken seriously. I need to complete an examination of what has so far been done.

The last days of my quarter of a century are not very eventful – a few deductions (how paltry), a couple of good poems – a surprising book – *Lord Jim*, but no essential information. Hardly wasting time anymore, that's something after all.

Australia doesn't want us, also America, hopefully they will be sorry one day. Something is missing, nothing makes sense.

Before the war many European Jews applied for entry to the United States. Its lure as a safe haven only grew once the war started. From behind barbed wire, many *Dunera* men continued to seek passage there, to no avail. American bureaucracy had ruled against accepting visa applications from internees. To apply one had first to be free. For internees dreaming of refuge, this seemingly perverse directive was a cruel blow.

FRIDAY 14 MARCH

Almost European with clouds, proper warm weather after weeks of boring blues and strongly fluctuating temperatures.

SATURDAY 15 MARCH

Meteorology – I'm increasingly sorry to have dropped it, though under the circumstances maybe it's lucky. I will never get much fun out of other subjects hereafter I'm afraid. Still, there is a lot to learn about dynamical Meteorology especially and physical dynamics by Vilhelm Bjerknes. Of all the many jobs I come to visualise these days, Meteorology seems brightest, even more than the aircraft industry or any other technical job with its dreary details and little thrill.

One day I will have to analyse the ten years from 1930 to 40 for myself, they are suitably sealed at each end for the purpose. This would mean concentrating, which has been long recognised as absolutely essential in view of the limited gifts I have received. So far no direction has been indicated, as I am fairly capable of learning almost anything, even without much inclination. I will have to be an engineer first for a time.

Anita Holper was a fellow internee. She was born in Italy in 1925 to Jewish Russian parents. Anita, her parents and elder brother fled to Singapore from Italy in 1938. In September 1940 they were arrested in Singapore as enemy nationals and deported on the *Queen Mary* to Australia, along with 262 other men, women and children, most of them Jews holding German or Italian passports. The *Queen Mary* docked at Sydney on 25 September 1940, after which these internees were taken to Tatura to be detained.
Photograph: Anita Holper, circa early 1940s.
Radok family collection.

TUESDAY 15 APRIL

Glorious day with work near the lake and a swim.

THURSDAY 17 APRIL

Anita goes tomorrow – a reason to write poetry.

WEDNESDAY 23 APRIL

Little taste of hunger – perhaps one would get used to it in time.

SATURDAY 26 APRIL

The Home Office man is finally here, and the first information is just as pessimistic as expected.

MONDAY 28 APRIL

The end of the Layton review of our application and we have a rejection for release in both Australia and England, na ja. My dreams became clearer; yesterday they were almost 'uncensored' about crawling through the fence with Anita on the other side.

Major Julian Layton was Liaison Officer for the British Home Office. His task was to attend to the *Dunera* internees' needs and to arrange for their release and repatriation. He arrived in Australia on 24 March 1941, and in April visited the *Dunera* internees at Hay, in New South Wales, and at Tatura. The Radok brothers did not warm to Layton.

THURSDAY 30 APRIL

Evening; it's still, like at the start of Carnival. I look away when really I should face it.

SATURDAY 3 MAY

My work efficiency is rather lowered by a fixation to Anita which is difficult to get out of. Still, perhaps it serves to keep one alive. Much is won by realising the reason for the decline of energy, where in earlier times I just noticed the effect and was disconcerted. Suppressing seems better when allowing a partial and unsatisfying outlet of imagination. Or recognising the intention without hiding it under a substitute – as up to now.

WEDNESDAY 14 MAY

All rather confused, even more than in reality. Another day of ambulant brooding produces and establishes the fact that I failed to do the right thing. Now there is no short-term chance. The whole thing reminds

Walter Wurzburger (1914–1995) was a Jewish musician and composer from Frankfurt. He was arrested and interned in Singapore in September 1940 on the basis of his German nationality, then deported to Australia on the *Queen Mary*. At Tatura he forged friendships with Uwe, and fellow *Queen Mary* internee Helmut Neustädter. This photograph of Wurzburger was taken in 1943.
Reproduced with the permission of the Wurzburger family.

vividly of puberty, thus spake Walter without realising fully what he said. However, we know more about it now, which is also why it must be difficult to get out of it. Some kind of sublimation is imperative and no more wasting time.

Many small incidents, perhaps of significance, perhaps there is an impending change of some sort?

THURSDAY 15 MAY

Experiment with libido.

FRIDAY 16 MAY

The outlook is rather gloomy and also personal; I do not know enough. My only chance is learning highly specialised theory in order to make a start in as many different directions as possible if Meteorology does not come off. It may be too late for aeronautics and actually it was always meant only as a bridge. Systematic work on maths. Language, Spanish to be continued and Russian taken up as soon as possible.

FRIDAY 23 MAY

The patient suffered anticipatory anxiety for a few days, the libido evaporated, just as required according to theory. Efficiency medium to low. New ideas about how to put things down – pro and contra suicide – however it's too theoretical to be of value, perhaps.

SATURDAY 24 MAY

For those who are going to England, it is getting serious and that stops any further discussion and unfortunately also the possibility of reading *Karamasoff*. I read *Tristram Shandi* instead. Math, without smoking, is moving forward, there really doesn't seem to be any nearby boundary. One difficulty after the next turns out to be smoke. I read a bad book by Huxley. I wonder whether one will be able to tolerate this harmlessness once more. At the moment, the setting alone – England without war – is unimaginable.

The first major exodus from internment of *Dunera* internees took place in June 1941. A total of 198 internees, from Hay and Tatura, sailed for Britain. Many of these men were released in Britain later that year.

Just take it as it happens and then act; save thinking for more important things.

SUNDAY 25 MAY

Departure of the returnees. The motives were probably very mixed. The thing that is constant is the need to do something which can be used to create the conditions for influence after the war. That pushes me towards the Pioneer Corps, but on the other hand there is the internal reason that I must stay here and other things that speak against it, the possibility of some worthwhile maths training, statistics etc.

FRIDAY 30 MAY

After some practice, letter writing slowly begins again. If there wasn't a war, it would be possible to continue studying, even if I were working in another field. My mistakes so far have always been in impatience instead of going slowly, so far in this way nothing has been achieved. Anita is gone and at the same time there is a new math course starting, although I will soon curse it.

THURSDAY 19 AND FRIDAY 20 JUNE

Layton is here again and the unrest that goes with his presence. There is no prospect for our release. The Pioneers are to go to England. Soon it will be time to decide. Morally and historically, everything speaks against it; the risk is great, there are a lot of rational points of view and the advantages if I am lucky and get through, are highly uncertain, like all promises. There is no possibility of continuing 'rational' training which is obviously necessary. At best, it's dull work with no illusions or ideals behind it. On the other hand, there is the fact that human development is almost impossible here, and that general development after the war will be made very difficult by the fact that I was 'not there'. On the other hand: will I ever have an influence on any particular area? Previously there has been a tendency to be too cautious but I wonder if that can be changed?

SUNDAY 22 JUNE

There's a rumour that there is news on the radio that Germany has declared war on Russia. Beginning of the end – or the end of a beginning?

TUESDAY 24 AND WEDNESDAY 25 JUNE

People believe that Russia will be over in 6 weeks. Some people will still be surprised.

THURSDAY 3 JULY

In the last few days I've had some insights into what it will be like. It is uncertain whether the Russians will make it. Although everyone has only become aware of it all, the world would be unspeakably empty if it ended unhappily – and everything would probably fail in the long run.

TUESDAY 15 JULY

The Russian Front is still standing. I got a Russian book, it's very difficult without grammar but useful in the long run. I've been in the joinery since yesterday and have already learned a lot. In contrast, this time I am more serious about it, I am old or at least older, and maths is not everything. I finally pulled myself together and worked out the Greek text of a Bible verse John 15/13 – so that you vent your rage against God and pour out such words from your mouth.

FRIDAY 18 JULY

One week of carpentry is over. I learned a lot and am undamaged by it. They are positive people so at least there is potential. Maths came up somewhat short, but that was to be expected at the beginning. Moreover, I notice I have grown a bit in the way I treat people. The overall mood is 'not bad', the Russians are holding out.

WEDNESDAY 23 JULY

I have a growing feeling of futility about everything in general and learning mathematics in particular. What good will it be in the post-war world which will be one of depression whatever shape it may take. I have an urge to write – but what and how?

Maybe I should just start – no matter if it becomes trite as it probably will. It would be off my chest, though. For example, write a play about the few worthwhile persons met in the last 1½ years.

SATURDAY 26 JULY

Carpentry is very satisfactory, the beautiful wood becomes like silk under the hand.

FRIDAY 1 AND SUNDAY 3 AUGUST

I have a new enthusiasm for glider construction, but it will not be completely forgotten again this time.

THURSDAY 7 AUGUST

We are meant to move, in the typical chicanery of the military authorities. Trying to stem the tide, even if objectively there is probably little hope for it. Slowly I come to realise what a stupid brutal lot civilians of all countries become when they put on uniforms.

Camp 3, Tatura.
Bern Brent collection.

SATURDAY 9 AUGUST

It will probably stay the same. I am fed up to the neck, not a lot of energy for anything. This sort of treatment reminds me again of the nonsense of our situation, especially because just today an engineer for Australia was released. Families are being torn apart, but a divorced husband who also wants to move has to go back to the other compound. The Home Office official doesn't step up to help; heaven only knows what he spends the time doing. Everything is a slimy mess that you cannot get out of, basically just like in a concentration camp. Na ja.

> Uwe was in Camp 3, Compound C. He was moved to Camp 4, Compound D. Wartime Tatura was home to an archipelago of internment camps. At different times four of these camps housed *Dunera* and *Queen Mary* internees. Who was held where, and when, is often unclear.

The fear of death is independent of knowledge of it. The animal has no knowledge of it and knows death, in spite of that. Compared with the time before you are born and after death – your lifetime is infinitesimally brief, so the importance and excitement attached to the problem of one's own death – to stay so long in the ground – seems absurd.

MONDAY 11 AUGUST

There is a growing tension about Japan. If there is going to be war, can we expect to be allowed to help or will we endure far more rigid restrictions regarding newspapers, letters, food etc? From our Australian experience up to now, the latter course would appear more probable even though there can't be anything in the nature of a real threat to this country for a long time to come. But Australians are aliens in their own country and not up to its size, perhaps that is the key to the whole muddle.

WEDNESDAY 13 AUGUST

Two editions of the *New Statesman* from May 1941 arrived. It seems England is already the way it used to be and the mood from the first days of the Churchill government has returned.

WEDNESDAY 20 AUGUST

After a few eventful days, things are slowly calming down again. Russian started and I should be able to finish the book I am reading in 3 months.

THURSDAY 21 AUGUST

Nerves are somewhat on the thin side at the moment, even the smallest triggers result in explosions. Ought to be stopped. I place 'home' over concentration camp in letter. There are people who were treated particularly badly every time the democracies expressed themselves compassionately, and now they sit behind the democratic barbed wire as dangerous enemy aliens, while outside the fight for justice and freedom is being fought. Redesign required.

FRIDAY 22 AUGUST

I had a surprising interview with someone who is looking for a physics teacher. Objectively it is out of the question, but a better impression wouldn't have hurt. At this point I notice how little is going on with me. The good ideas catch up regularly. The mistake is that I can't really do anything completely; then like in roulette, I could wait for the number to come up. It is constantly changing and none of the many partial competencies are enough. Where that is meant to lead, who knows?

SATURDAY 23 AUGUST

Listening to records, Bach, Mozart, Bach double concerto is meant to be particularly impressive. It will remain that way. For a few years after the war, only Bach will be played.

I have a discussion with Walter about the never-ending question of what I actually want, i.e. what I would do if I could do whatever I wanted. With him it is clear – on the other hand, the one time something was felt, it didn't feel quite convincing on this side.

TUESDAY 26 AUGUST

The shortage of time is becoming more and more noticeable or is it the increase in topics? Now it's easy to understand why I didn't get anywhere outside as there was too much there, and I had no special talents or imbalance to make the choices easier. However, this being so, something has got to happen about it.

THURSDAY 28 AUGUST

I made an unsuccessful attempt to write to Ian's 'superiorly' – I am so poisoned by the constant confrontation with the quagmire that the poison comes through at every opportunity.

I should get it off my chest once and for all– but how? In reality, it indicates I still believe other conditions to be <u>possible</u> despite evidence and my own evidence to the contrary. If I could realise that this is how it must be under the present system or world, I could be thorough and maybe look for a way to alter it.

THURSDAY 4 SEPTEMBER

Ian has now joined up to the Royal Air Force. My attempt to write has so far failed. It comes to an intolerable stammering. Interview outside but my success is questionable, it can't do any damage either. I am already in danger of getting too used to this life anyway.

TUESDAY 9 SEPTEMBER

Began *Brothers Karamazov* a few days ago, a fantastic book.

FRIDAY 12 SEPTEMBER

Finished *Karamazov*. If I had written something like that, I might be satisfied, which shows the impossibility of the matter. If I take a closer look, I have already experienced most of it or can imagine what it is like, except for one thing. If it came to that, then what? An active life perhaps without much illusion about its importance. We are more the objects of a legal process than subjects whose intentions matter. That holds true for everyone including those who are believed to 'make' history, e.g. Roosevelt. Today's speech was understandable from his standpoint, but it is equally clear that the other side must oppose it. The personal closeness through the radio only reinforces the impression that there is actually not that big a difference between him and us – 'he is on the wheel too'.

There was resignation in the hope that justice will be done some time, precisely now that it is clear that this word means nothing in an inhuman history. The logic looks something like this: we are interned as Nazis, so long as the war is only against Nazism. Rehabilitated and kept shut up as Germans after the war, meanwhile switched to being against the Germans themselves. After the war things will revert to the first hypothesis, we are Nazis because we were interned. There will be no justice and right in that moment, one feels compelled to mention it. If I were in the UK now, it would not be better, but it would occasionally be 'fun'. Work in England would be the most endurable existence.

MONDAY 15 SEPTEMBER

Evening: I wrote a mischievous letter about certain petty problems and intelligence practices and feel nice and warm after it. This tone is much more useful than grumbling. However, this did mean giving up hope for change. One of the things that I would have to get used to would be the return to Germany.

FRIDAY 19 SEPTEMBER

There are new rumours, of a pretty reliable nature, that things are heading somewhere else again. If only I was at the point where it did not matter. The '*Arandora* problem' has not yet been touched on in any way and I would be just as helpless as on the *Dunera*. Dona nobis pacem, but that does not exist, as nice and fundamental as the idea of the phrase is. If only I was able to really get clarity about everything and write it down.

FRIDAY 26 SEPTEMBER

The second anniversary of our arrest passed without anything significant happening – everything remains as plans. Occasionally, in conversation, things come out that previously were not clear – continuations of painstakingly captured trains of thought. But that is the only way so far. Perhaps I will get writing.

SATURDAY 27 SEPTEMBER

Aid for Russia is intentionally slack? The Japanese situation is slowly but surely approaching war. Our release is apparently only via the Pioneer Corps. Light – failed.

WEDNESDAY 1 OCTOBER

I have been feeling rather depressed, assisted by too many cigarettes during the last few days. In addition, a release and the announcement of an England transporter – which we should be on, even if it doesn't look as if it will be possible for us. I have made fruitless attempts to express something over the last few days in conversations with Rainer. If only one could find a substitute for a conversation. Letters don't do it, there is a lack of proximity or perhaps dissent as well. Since it only works in exceptional cases, it could also depend on the recipient.

SUNDAY 5 OCTOBER

New people have arrived, an Australian sailor and two enterprising boys, one serious and pleasant, whose time R. monopolised. R. is writing a book, likely in the form of a novel about his generation that has missed out. I want to see the conclusions. But it fits. I can't get anyone to look deeper, to look for the root of things as they are instead of showing why they ought to be otherwise. 'Of pleasure and pain he knows, and deems it something strange when he is other than glad'. I am rather sure that is not the way.

TUESDAY 7 OCTOBER

At times there is a concrete feeling that I understand why things are as they are and at other times it's more likely I am the sewer of pants who thought 'all of the above was fun'. Still, it seems that this was always the problem in the strange interviews in Seaton and that it is the reason why I didn't and don't find any topics of conversation with most people. There's a new story, beginning with *Arandora* or equivalent and before that, long before, but looking back at my own strange self. ('We are too young to fall to dust and too unsatisfied to die'. *Ballad of Heaven*, Davidson).

Excerpt from Uwe's interview with the British Advisory Committee to Consider Appeals against Orders of Internment, 5 January 1940.
Questioner: Would you contemplate returning to Germany, for example, if better times came to Germany?
Uwe: I said at my first interrogation I intended to go back for my honeymoon but not otherwise.
Questioner: Were you looking forward to your honeymoon?
Uwe: No, it was to illustrate it was very, very improbable.
Questioner: Of course, humour is a dangerous thing in Scotland.
Source: TNA (UK), HO 382/541.

SATURDAY 11 OCTOBER

I finished the *Reader's Digest* review after days of rest. My review is written in English and there is little satisfaction because of that. I read an article by Stephen Spender on *Books and the War*. It is worthy of notice and a more thorough investigation. My ideas about what to write are getting more numerous – it feels rather like the moment before orgasm. I took a side look into *Truth about France*; the military details are rather confusing. It is like trying to understand the exact happenings during the end of a test, the actual cracking – whereas useful information is usually derived from the knowledge of load and initial diameter only, the initial conditions which can be completely understood.

SUNDAY 12 OCTOBER

How far can things be explained by a combination of the facts that the individual consciousness and life depend on the libido (Freud) and the level of production (Marx)?

TUESDAY 14 OCTOBER

I made a mess of the carpentry problem – I am no better in that respect than before. The only development appears to be in regard to consciousness of myself and things around. But I am not going to be a great success at that, I can't imagine a normal life as an engineer, perhaps Meteorology, if anything. I am more likely to become a failure for the price of realising some of the reasons why things are as they are.

THURSDAY 16 OCTOBER

I read the *Grapes of Wrath*, it is like *Co-op* but much better, except for the finish which is slightly kitsch and besides does not finish the book in the least. It is consoling to know it was beyond the author's power to find a general end to that story! If only I could write that chapter. There is enormous significance in the fact that books like that are written.

I had an argument with Jobst who accuses me of not making use of my handicap in the 'family' interest. He is not quite wrong there – I am apt to hold back having come to a slight understanding of what is going on outside. And everything normal up to now has rather lost importance lately. Kaczynski's remark that the invention to make sand of air, though being a remarkable feat, would not be of much consequence if made in the Sahara. If only I could stop being at odds with myself. If I was released today, it might be fatal with so much undischarged and not understood energy. At any rate, a complacent life can't come back under the circumstances, but dying would be hard to face now. Somehow it seems to have become increasingly so with the years. Seeing there are only two problems, and this is the most urgent

Gerhard Kaczynski (1920–1983) was a farm worker and stove fitter from Berlin.

one at present, I should get down to it now, so as to leave a free man should the chance arise. All rather muddled.

FRIDAY 17 OCTOBER

Smoking too much – that may be the reason for the decline. Try to stop it.

All writers are more or less faced by the same problem; talk about high causes has gone far enough, one must tell the truth about the intolerable suffering which one sees.

SATURDAY 18 OCTOBER

I had a dream about houses of cards that collapsed. But the evening before, I had an idea about how to lay the thing out.

Two precious years of freedom from purpose and freedom from freedom itself. I've been relieved from all accustomed surroundings and influences and people, and forced to realise my dependence on sexual energies at last. It can't last much longer – or may continue for years. In both cases it will be different from now. This is the time for reckoning, to find what I could and what I would want to do and to realise those things in which I am continually failing. To get something to live for if I am to live – and to get a view of things to die with, if I am to die. To have the certain knowledge that nothing that I could do matters once I am gone. If it is good, somebody else would have found it and the only difference would be the loss of thrill to have been in the frontline. Discoveries will leave a stale taste and formula and laws will lose their spell despite the lust of finding them. No wonder people can't find war aims just now; how many of them have any life aims? The prospect of becoming a failure in manifold ways arises very clearly on this occasion. There is no doubt of a certain analytical gift, particularly in the criticism of my own ideas and accomplishments which cannot be silenced, just as the instinctive attempt to understand the adversary's point of view.

The world is out of joint – I wish I knew whether I was born to set it right or help doing so.

This cannot be decided now, though it would be good to prepare for the usual type of life, ending perhaps in the least drab of all lives open to those born without creative faculties or too much self-criticism or single mindedness.

Still, all this may be the result of the lack of an outlet for sexual energies, and their urgency tends to diminish when this problem is finally resolved. Then I may not be altogether happy with the rest of the new knowledge which cannot be forgotten.

SUNDAY 19 OCTOBER

This is primarily interesting from a psychological standpoint as a young man. The sexually dependent part is kept secret, and that of economics is completely below the threshold of consciousness. The rational training of mathematics is excellent as soon as you start to use it elsewhere.

Vergil, Huxley and the rest, should be consulted before I try to put into words my own idea about it. But that isn't the problem here; at any rate there emerges and remains, even after most illusions have fallen during the two years of analysing opportunity, the fact of our dependency on sex and economics more than on anything else. If it is remembered that there is nothing final to be gained by science alone, the question arises: what is to be done?

I would like to be a lasting influence but honestly the mettle isn't there for it.

What should I do? Satisfaction and happiness may hereafter have to be bound up with other than intellectual accomplishments of which so far little is known, while 'the world as I see it' does not offer much chance for satisfaction. Analysis of certain periods: fear of no success. There is a chance of being gifted for teaching. Dreaming of ideas for the present is all that can be done. It's a poor life to look back on. What experiences were squandered by being blind at their time?

MONDAY 20 OCTOBER

It turns out now that what looked like an impulse for creative work was really an intolerable undernourishment of certain parts and thus revolt against the rest. For weeks now everything else has laid idle, including at the end, even Russian. Perhaps restraint on other planes is just as effective as on the sexual one, if intensive enough.

TUESDAY 21 OCTOBER

I give things a rest for one day. There is plenty to do, Russian and maths, though the first is more important and can be done almost as a whole spare time job here.

Believe it or not – though the result seems meagre, and without having read it again, there seems to have been a success of some sort as far as clearing the brain is concerned. A 2-month-old problem has been solved almost at the first attempt – in a rather obvious way, which however failed to occur then.

I'm feeling rather elated about it, rather real physically. Looking back, I can almost remember the different thoughts 'dropping in', I ought to ease the crest of the wave for similar questions to verify if it is real.

Evening – music with little concentration, is it because of that?

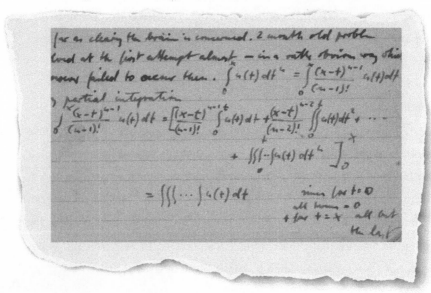

WEDNESDAY 24 OCTOBER

All experiences are imaginable, except one – is it worth waiting for it? For all its insistency there ought to be something in it, only no clue is given as to how to do it. Should I learn maths and languages and hope for the best? Need to not get into a fix again, to keep an open mind? Very bad at dying for things or ideas and perhaps less for persons. Few things and no ideas seem to be worth it after all.

I'm rather fed up with lectures, every time I feel a considerable fatigue at the slightest prospect of striking home. I've lost a good deal of mental mobility; it's hard to get going on a problem. With carpentry I'm frequently fed up to the neck, but I am going to stick to it. It is likely to be the one great asset of this period, to have something I can put my hands to. It's part of repairing the starved portion of myself. So too is playing the violin in a quartet, it's also somewhat gratifying to realise my possibilities but it's not going to become much of an occupation though I'll have some practice.

SATURDAY 25 OCTOBER

Restless. It seems to be in the same line as a feeling of illness two days ago, together with a wish to leave everything for some time and just do nothing. But it isn't worth it – I need to keep a grip on it. The observation by Lawrence is interesting in this connection, probably one could control a good deal of real illness.

Why am I still hovering over the idea to write down how I believe things to be connected? It won't help very much towards using this knowledge instinctively and acting accordingly – that is a question of time and ageing. But to think out how things ought to be may be worthy of notice. After all, I am a fairly average example – I've no special ingeniousness, just normal gifts, which may be more accentuated in one or the other direction.

MONDAY 27 OCTOBER

Our appeal for reclassification has been denied. 'If you want to corrupt an honest man, call him a liar'. At least, now it is clear what to do – and that it will take a long time. There is more chance for fighting the issue on this moral plane and it will be more satisfactory too if we are successful. Nevertheless, I have to realise that success will be just luck since it would not be caused by reasonable consideration by the Home Office, but by coincidence of good words put in by influential people, a good breakfast and what not.

Cuttings have been sent to Norman Birkett and Morrison and to Holmes, explaining why it is not the Labour office for us and asking for maths courses.

In the afternoon news came that we were to be transferred to the Nazis' section, our reaction obvious.

TUESDAY 28 OCTOBER

I am still rather affected by the black day before, the only bright spot was the double concerto for two violins by Bach. Letters with sound and fury, somewhat sharper this time. The result remains to be seen. Firstly, I must expect a transfer and trouble. It is awful that I cannot think of anything other than what the lights will be like while hearing good music, a Mozart violin concerto on the wireless. That is where this damnable injustice gets me. If the man who is responsible in the head office had shown his own anti-fascism half as often as we have during these two years I should be surprised. Still, we are their slaves. Maybe these are still the effects of the *Arandora Star*, Jobst is rather emphatic and convinced on that point.

WEDNESDAY 29 OCTOBER

Trying to get through the *Bible of the World* before Friday.

Rest rather in a hurry but nothing special in it. Hunting for ethics rather than for religion of which there is plenty. Besides plenty to occupy my mind.

THURSDAY 30 OCTOBER

Opening the boil. At any rate it can't do any harm to leave no secret shadows.

It's a rather awkward situation when I come to think of it, seeing the tendency is to be found almost everywhere and it is very difficult to get rid of the suspicion therefore. It is one 'moving' force I did not really dream of before being interned.

FRIDAY 31 OCTOBER

Alex has been released; it's slowly emptying. The lowest point ought to have now been crossed and an ascent slowly beginning again with the effective prevention of us being sent to join the Nazis in the camp. We still have to expect that we will get away and that it will be a long time before we put everything behind us.

Alex was possibly Alexander Marx (1903–1984), a company director from Frankfurt. He had left Tatura in early October and sailed for Ecuador on the 12th of that month.

SATURDAY 1 NOVEMBER

I listen to the Bach concert with awareness, it's an exhausting piece of music.

Afternoon thermal, seagulls climb to 500m in 1–2 minutes. I take an evening walk with Walter and try to talk about my own half-finished ideas, unsuccessfully, as expected.

TUESDAY 6 NOVEMBER

I transferred the *Dunera* records into this diary, they are somewhat depressing in their continual expression of only one thought. But then, I remember distinctly that there were others too. Layton is here; a business confirmed. I am rather disgusted but then we pretended to see things in their true light all along and it has just become as bad as could be expected. We must reckon with being moved too, though not to the Nazis. Our program is to make the Home Office reopen this injustice, or else we'll have to beat it somehow.

I am reading a book on Meteorology, for the first time something really complete, advanced and useful.

FRIDAY 7 NOVEMBER

There are plenty of things on hand – Suitcase, Letters, Meteorology, Russian and Maths. It feels not unlike the dreams of past times when one was desperately trying to catch up with somebody on a train. Still, for the sake of experiment, we'll try it a few more days. The main features are a desire to lie down and forget about everything and sleep, especially after glancing at what is to be done and what I would like to do. The Japanese situation is still uncertain; today again a 'silver lining' of clouds. However, unless the Russian war takes a sudden turn for the good, war is inevitable.

SUNDAY 9 NOVEMBER

Yesterday we had an excursion, nice, wide country. Soaring birds, pelicans? Must be great flying here. In the evening I listened to Beethoven 133 and Mozart D minor string quartet fugue. It is the end of the idle time. As long as there is a chance of learning something in the carpentry shop, we've got to stick to it. Lectures are no good since there is nobody interested, just as in math, which will perhaps be discontinued after the exams. There is more sense in helping individuals, Rainer say, with complex ideas. A collection has been taken up for the Russian Red Cross – the first time we have an opportunity to take part.

MONDAY 10 NOVEMBER

There is a wire from Norman Birkett. He has 'made enquiries, did you volunteer for Pioneers?' That means it is still true that the only way out is the Pioneer Corps, now that it has been shown that they don't trust or accept us. But that may change and it's in our hands to make that happen in the foreseeable future. The outcomes are decided by other people or, probably, other factors.

In the northern winter of 1939-40, the eminent British lawyer Norman Birkett presided over a tribunal at which the three Radok brothers appealed unsuccessfully against their internment. Evidently, Birkett maintained an interest in their fortunes.

Just as I come to realise now some of the benefits of internment, the need for solving my own problems before I attempt to solve others, a key for politics perhaps.

There is plenty alluring in the thought of getting away from here to whatever kind of life. We'll have to fight it out with the Home Office. Being a skilled worker or farm hand would not require discussion.

SATURDAY 15 NOVEMBER

I'm rather mentally deficient all the time, the reason is rather obvious when I try to inform friends of the new Home Office developments and cannot stop myself getting into a white heat rage. So, I had better drop the subject for some time yet. It's an unpleasant condition not to be able to think out the easiest maths problem. If that should ever become a sign of ageing it will mean a great crisis, it is just a half-life without this facility.

THURSDAY 20 NOVEMBER

I've had a few ideas about the value of intellectual commitments, scientific or math, for maintaining my mental balance under probably almost any condition. I have a tendency to cynicism regarding the objectively much more important happenings elsewhere, on account of my own unjust fate. My preference is for a sleeping state – where colours and everything can seem at least as distinct as in waking and memory from each sense of being half-awakened, the waves of sleep reproducing the spell for moments.

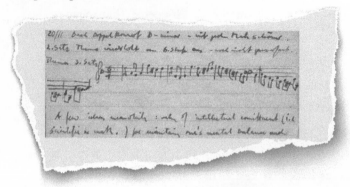

FRIDAY 21 NOVEMBER

I had a dream about Rainer who was indignant about some delay in telegrams coming; unmistakeably sexual, confirming the earlier instance. There is a note of sadness, there are plenty of new rumours after yesterday's arrival of Free French Legionnaires. But it leaves me rather cold. I'm waiting for the end of lectures next week to start Meteorology – and Russian, which has been neglected lately. After that we'll see further – 'for I have conquered fate'. Mood – veering towards optimism.

MONDAY 24 NOVEMBER

Vanity is beautiful – that's a new one. I need to try to instil Walter with a little more self-confidence, rightly so too.

THURSDAY 27 NOVEMBER

I meddled again with other people's affairs and forced a quartet rehearsal. In spite of all circumstances objecting, the result was unsatisfactory for all who matter. Afterwards I had no urge for anything, Meteorology was too difficult for just reading. My thoughts are inexpressible, probably there aren't any.

It's gradually developing to a state where modern music alone is bearable besides Bach and earlier. Everything between – late Beethoven quartets are an exception, and there may be a few others – is just as superfluous as most books of the normal novel type.

FRIDAY 28 NOVEMBER

Wittke is off to England. There are rumours that all English internees are soon to follow in *Dunera* fashion mostly likely. I must try to get through with Meteorology, as difficult as it is with carpentry and the heat. News item of yesterday – Morrison attacked on 18B, disregard of Aliens' Committee recommendation in nearly 150 cases, a full victory for him after his threat to resign. There is frustration at growing number of detentions if the invasion danger is revived. I have a feeling our case may have contributed to this discussion, unfortunately no text is given.

Valentin Wittke (1904–1975) was a joiner and cabinetmaker from Marienburg, Germany. He left Tatura on 28 November 1941, and sailed for Britain on 12 December.

Of course, there is not much sense in returning if the position is like that. I have a desire for normal life which maybe will never come under the circumstances. Growing urge to express it.

SATURDAY 29 NOVEMBER

Plenty of mail from the family. There is a palpable disappointment from them about our lack of contact except from Rainer. The dream of coming home is also there. If we actually have to, or are allowed to go back, I will have to write openly for once.

SUNDAY 30 NOVEMBER

The edge of the new good spirit has been revived by a cool change, but the program is mostly finished, lectures, trunk, jumping pit.

WEDNESDAY 5 DECEMBER

I happily calculated a rather tricky derivative for the first time in a while – vector analysis. Otherwise, I have been turning over the points for and against returning to England in a new *Dunera*. First one is that it seems suicidal, second, it is rather unreasonable in view of the long-term development of the war. Fatalism is not much good under the circumstances.

Japan not exacerbated, apparently they are waiting for the takeover of the French fleet. Really, we are doing far too well here, with this constancy and relative security. However, today has been quiet. At first, I was worried with second thoughts. Perhaps, after all, I am going to meet or am meant to meet somebody somewhere – half of life maybe not yet gone – maybe.

I had an evening discussion with Ro in the coffeehouse. He is always a very suitable counterpart, I can be sure of a serious and 'intelligent', if screwy, reception for my brainchild. His theory of long-term development to be compared with Fernkraft theory.

MONDAY 8 DECEMBER

News has come that Japan has bombed Manila so what they were waiting for all the time must have happened at last, Libia or Russian or French fleet or whatever it was.

Communication will be difficult again, perhaps; it is too late now to do something about it, to give some substance for living on. I am feeling very egotistical but how could it have been different. Our removal is not very likely now, at least not overseas. Maybe to other camps, or tents, or just no radio and newspapers and camps filled up. Never mind – it was obvious that we are still on the downward trend. Our volunteering for the Australian Army is not likely to come off soon. It is no good to overdo it and to lose the 'cup'.

'ah my beloved, fill the cup that clears
Today of past regrets and future fears.'

— TATURA, 1941 —

WEDNESDAY 10 DECEMBER

The war news is bad, the militant form of decaying capitalism knows better what they want than the others. Maybe everything is going to bits too completely to start the new system.

MONDAY 15 DECEMBER

Very hot lately – mental activity thus curtailed.

Looks like we will be marching off to the Labour Corps soon, but of course it can take years.

Sometimes I ought to be able to paint: yesterday the dust storm over the camp with the lone gigantic 'dishevelled' tree. I must try to do it sometime.

The *Dunera* internee Robert Hofmann (1889–1987) was a professional artist of renown. This sketch is thought to date from 1941.
Reproduced courtesy of the Jewish Museum of Australia, and with the permission of Mark Topp and James Skvarch.
Untitled, Robert Hofmann, c. 1941, Tatura, pastel on paper, 310 x 247mm. Donated by Jimmy King. Jewish Museum of Australia collection 7035.

THURSDAY 18 DECEMBER

Anne Lindburgh's *North to the Orient* – not yet read except the preface where she draws the necessity to write her story as a passing storm which was possible only for a few years and will no longer be possible after this war anyway. But something more important is shown in it too: the result of the book was a personal satisfaction to her belonging

to the people who like to recount their adventures, the diary keepers, the story tellers, the letter-writers, a strange race of people who feel half cheated of an experience unless it is retold. It does not really exist until it is put into words. As though a little doubting or dull, they could not see it until it is repeated. For 'paradoxically enough' the more unreal an experience becomes – translated from real action into unreal words, dead symbols for life itself – the more vivid it grows. Now actually it would be strange if otherwise since the symbols are all we have in consciousness. Not only does it seem more vivid, but its essentials become clearer. One says excitedly to an audience 'do you see – I can't tell you how it was – we all of us felt' although actually, at the time of the incident, one was not conscious of such a feeling, and only became so in the retelling.

Perhaps it is also the growing disillusions against the childish hope of suddenly getting out of it all, back into the comfortability of before, which of course still persists in some way. Some of it is gone though; there is a disappointment at not belonging to the first list of release for industry candidates.

There is only the one letter, thought of some time ago when going back to England was still possible. It is the most difficult one and last to be written – if at all.

THURSDAY 25 DECEMBER

It's very hot – little energy, even Meteorology losing its appeal at times. Besides there are signs of another period of symptoms pointing to libido starvation; rational work alone is insufficient in the long run, as was to be expected. Control is impossible without tons of material and books – perhaps later.

SATURDAY 27 DECEMBER

It is still very hot. Carpenter work outside. I finished history; the early part somewhat too vain. When not working I wait for the weather to change. Last night it looked like the beginning but turned out to be a 'local incident' after all.

All evening Walter sat in a deckchair under a Japanese like moon and tree combination. I am trying to produce real memories, doubtful of success, probably owing to a lack of technique in description.

Why is it things that I feel completely sure about get blurred when I try to put them into words for others?

TATURA, 1942

THURSDAY 1 JANUARY

Sylvester with Show – I was somehow in the mood and liked it. In general, there is the feeling that the last year was quite successful in many ways with a shortening of the lines and taking up old, prepared positions, so to speak, which can be equal to getting older. I have an increasing interest in humanity which is not as fluctuating as before, including the new food by Finnish internees who don't fit into the internment pattern in the least.

Sylvester (commonly Silvester) is the German name for New Year's Eve.

What is wrong with me seems to be still the same – no end in view.

THURSDAY 8 JANUARY

Spirits are not particularly high these days. There is talk of a new Nazi departure, so there will be a number of 'mistakes', no doubt, again. *Toccata and Fugue* by Wurzburger.

There is a change in my opinion expressed to Ian in August '39 shortly before everything started, that we can't expect decent happenings before all people have somehow become decent, as opposed to today's opinion that firstly we must create the right material conditions to make one decent.

MONDAY 12 JANUARY

The feeling of resentment at being classified as a Nazi is rather active again, with corresponding consequences on the correspondence.

THURSDAY 15 JANUARY

Practising Walter's *Toccata and Fugue* with great enjoyment, the first time for years on the piano.

SUNDAY 18 JANUARY

Yesterday, after 3 weeks reconsideration, the reply came that we would be going to England. There is the expected turmoil of pro and contra after the decision to accept. The wheel slowly starts up again and immediately the whole outlook becomes blurred. It will be a hard time for our family in America. This thought spoils all personal satisfaction in the face of this chance, even though we have made the decision.

The reference to family in the United States is to Uwe's parents, Fritz and Gertrud, and his sister Gundula, who had arrived in New York in February 1941, having fled Europe.

Early in the war there was a widespread desire among many *Dunera* internees to return to Britain, usually as soon as Major Layton could facilitate their transport. On 12 January 1942, the Radok brothers were given approval to travel to Britain, where officials would consider their cases and decide whether to grant their freedom. The approval became moot. Japan's entry into the Second World War in December 1941 had complicated the return of internees, not least because transport had become harder to obtain. From June to December 1941, eight ships carrying *Dunera* internees left Australia bound for Britain. The next ship to do so did not depart until July 1942. By that stage the Radok brothers had enlisted in the Australian Army.

From the United States, Fritz had petitioned the
Australian Prime Minister to release his sons.

TELEPHONE No.: CANBERRA 531.
TELEGRAPHIC ADDRESS: "PRIMISTER," CANBERRA.
CABLE ADDRESS: "KINDLIER," CANBERRA.

COMMONWEALTH OF AUSTRALIA.

PRIME MINISTER'S DEPARTMENT.

Canberra, 25th September, 1941.

In reply quote No. G.20/1/2.

3 XI.

Dear Sir,

I am directed by the Prime Minister to acknowledge the
receipt of your recent letter regarding your three sons, Uwe, Jobst
and Rainer Radok, internees transferred from the United Kingdom for
internment in Australia, and to inform you that internees from the
United Kingdom were accepted for internment only, and cannot normally
be released in Australia. In the event of their release being
authorised by the United Kingdom Authorities, they will be returned
to the United Kingdom, or permitted to proceed to some neutral
country to which they can secure admission, as may be directed.

An application for release from internment made by your
sons has been referred to the appropriate United Kingdom authorities
who have advised that the Secretary of State could find no sufficient
ground for authorising their release. This decision has been
conveyed to your sons.

In view of the above circumstances, I am to express regret
that the Commonwealth Government is not in a position to authorise
the release of your sons from internment.

Yours faithfully,

F. Strahan

Secretary.

F. Radok, Esq.,
      C/- Miss Valentine,
          210 South Avenue,
              New Canaan, Conn., U.S.A.

Letter to Fritz Radok from Frank Strahan, Secretary, Prime Minister's Department.
Radok family collection.

MONDAY 19 JANUARY

So far, I am unable to convince myself that all this is to be real and serious.

Now it seems to me that I had come across Him on a few occasions, even though I can't say I met Him face to face then as last time. The first occasion must have been during one of my first flights in tow by an aeroplane when the release mechanism failed to open as it should have. Later occasions were when spinning down on to a hard, frozen ground at Munich, in winter 1934; at Nidden in a glider after having ventured out too far into the sea during stormy weather; and finally in Scotland, a few months before the war, during a flight which ended in my first actual crash.

On all these occasions there was, for a short time, a feeling of imminent fundamental crisis. But all these occasions passed without leaving any lasting impressions, which must have been due to the relatively low level of consciousness I had reached until quite lately. The war did not make much difference then, and a weak attempt at understanding it thoroughly did not get anywhere. Then there came the *Arandora* episode, destroying for some time all possibilities for sleep in a great flash, leaving one dazzled by its significance. To complete the impression, it was followed by the seven weeks of transport to Australia during which, almost continuously, all requirements were fulfilled for completing the first unsuccessful attempt to confront Him without any danger of failing again. I might have fallen asleep again after the first flash, but as it was, the sequel kept me awake and aware of what it meant; at the time we were not on equal terms, and I never got beyond wishing for the opportunity to prepare for a next time.

But all the time the problem waited in the background, outside the barbed wire so to speak, sure to get its own again some time, and it had to be faced, particularly after there came growing evidence that it will be a familiar question for years to come, long after this, when in the purely military sense it will have been finished.

At first, I could only plead that, after all, the main feelings had not been fear, but the horror of vacui, the thought of being cut off suddenly from all the things still to be done and to be enjoyed. This naturally led to investigating – there is no getting past one's scientific training and instincts – these things to be done and to be enjoyed.

SUNDAY 25 JANUARY

A few days earlier, on 21 January, Frank Forde, Minister for the Army, had announced that internees would be able to enlist in an unarmed labour company of the Australian Army. In this way freedom could be secured.

Yesterday the return to England was 'postponed indefinitely'. We worked out a new policy between the new Labour Corps and returning, maybe splitting our forces would be more sensible than risking the lot again. No great heat put up for anything – things will develop the way they want at any rate.

My attempt to sum up is rather futile, maybe on account of trying to do it literature-like or in English which is only usable for straightforward statements so far.

TUESDAY 27 JANUARY

Two days ago, 'no drive' – again an indescribable impression.

Yesterday I did easy work in the MI office and had a hard struggle to decide myself for or against Labour Corps. While in a way I should like to return to Europe, the prospect of being a relatively free person in a few days is very enticing.

Though it seems unlikely, given the context of internment, MI in this context probably stands for Military Intelligence. The Army was short of interpreters and may have asked certain internees to help translate routine documents containing no sensitive information.

Finally, we decided to make a bid for it and failed today. The same Home Office which can classify as B somebody else who always was a Nazi, and can let them join up, cannot make up its mind to let us join. Thus, the only solution to turn our whole internment from a long chain of stupidity into something sensible, has been shattered again by purely bureaucratic objections, and we remain interned – though slightly burnt. It feels very much like having decided to make a run for a bus one somehow knew one should not reach beforehand – and missing it.

SATURDAY 31 JANUARY

Change has come after all, quite a pleasant experience one should have missed if the Labour affair had come off. New people, mainly young scientists and engineers but some of them are not so sure either, it seems. You can see from their eyes whether they have been working in their subject all along or played Bridge or crossed a 'shadow line'.

I have a tendency to be attracted by every clean-cut young face, which is not very difficult to understand, but at any rate there is nothing doing. I expected to find young S of the *Dunera* here, but he went away before. Thus, I can't expect that I know anyone else.

At any rate, nothing any longer is able to make me lose my temper, which is a lot. There is a prospect of getting carpenter work again, in partnership with somebody of apparently some shadow line experience, Fred G, a prevented student of architecture. Nothing ever went according to the first impression.

> The mathematician was almost certainly Dr Felix Behrend (1911–1962) from Berlin. He was released from Tatura in March 1942 to work as a mathematician at the University of Melbourne.

There is a Dr of math and despite it, quite human; unfortunately, he is just about to leave for Melbourne, he could have got me out of the present deadlock otherwise.

TUESDAY 3 FEBRUARY

All books dropped for the time being – just living for human things of which there are a number. On top of it, still the same Fred G and it turned out that it was no first impression after all. He came to our table on the first evening to take down names, an incident I can distinctly remember having been naturally very attentive during that time. But I have no recollection whatever, that it was the same face which afterwards impressed me with 'eyes quite on the edge of the head'. He is young and shy, in a difficult position not having been able to finish or carry on his studies of architecture for the lack of money. Now he, as others, is wavering between returning and the Pioneer Corps. He is very easily impressed, 'too soon made glad', and somewhat on high tension. Working together did not come off – I'm not so very sorry having experienced it for one afternoon. But with all sorts of strategies and ruses, we can have walks and a few discussions, the danger of dominating too much so far mostly avoided.

Everything else has lost much of its importance and I only live for the present state which is bound to be short I'm afraid. But even then, there is something left out in the previous considerations.

The state of just being glad to be in somebody's presence, without attempting as formerly to take much influence and to look for aims, the one result of having crossed a shadow line if it was one. And the reason, which is not very difficult to guess, does not make any difference – shall we say yet? There is bound to be some reaction about the fact that all the accumulated intensity of years comes out this way. But it does come out and it is hopeless to attempt to stop it.

I'm trying to get a picture of the group of young scientists who all are rather impressive and can show human sides to a large extent, besides being at 20 or 21 far beyond my own knowledge of their subjects. The method of succession approximations, seeing them through other people's eyes.

WEDNESDAY 4 FEBRUARY

Last night I tried to get Fred to come for a walk, but he did not take the hint and I did not force it, sensibly, 'to yield with a grace to reason'. I went off alone, rather inspired by having made use of this difficulty in a moment to bind things over to the next day. Even the prospect of what I am going to say today is sufficient, although I didn't in the end. Thus, nearness must not be taken literally.

The feeling of being subject to absolute physical law is strong again – one has to meet somebody and be in a position to notice him – the rest is bound to the wheel. Earlier events of this kind appear to have been somehow 'without energy' – the current following voltage at such an angle as to use up no energy or not to produce any. Increasing consciousness has diminished the angle this time – I won't say brought it to zero.

A classification of all cases up to now would probably yield as a result the fact that there have been two sorts, resulting in attachment of different intensity for some reason. This one is of the interior kind, an unconscious beginning? Walter would be at the other end with the intensity stronger on his side.

What is to be done? Rational subjects are no good here. As it is, this is bound to be more than transient. I wonder if he'd be more open for it, once it can be told.

Physical reality is fundamental even if we realise that it is an illusion for others.

FRIDAY 6 FEBRUARY

Two days ago there was a perfect evening and we had a long talk, not one-sided. My diagnosis has been fairly correct. He has a bad memory, but it seems only for things that were not yet meant for him. I got somewhat hot myself over the question of the effect of sexual abstinence. There is a new fact or maybe axiom which is slightly overstated, that one must either show signs of repression and discontentment here or else suffer atrophic changes in some way.

The next day we spent working together in the morning. It was quite different except there was a general nearness, I believe on both sides. In the afternoon I was working alone giving some indication of what the time afterwards will be. All nails were bent over, impatient, disgusted.

But it seems we are going to remain a repair gang somewhat longer. As an architect he is increasingly tied up in our job and Mr S's skill in cutting me out is all right with me. I can't blame him since I have little enough real interest in the work. Today again Fred was only partly at the job, but he shows enough interest to believe in duration. In the evening we played hand ball – a nervy bunch but plucky enough.

'He that has once been happy, he can bear to die', 'but the poet lies too much'. I can already see now that it will have been our moment at some peak afterwards – which might just as well never have been at all. The only way for continuity may still turn out to be working together – sharing not only a few momentary thoughts, but a spell and obsession.

It can't be complete purposelessness like this now. So, I'll be in the old way before long – seeing no completeness will arise in this case, maybe a few more talks before the last one. I'd like to help him, it should be possible after having been in similar troubles not long ago, though to some extent it is too recent for me to be quite sure how I got out of them.

'What has this to do with love
The anguish and sharp despair
The madness roving in the blood
Because a girl or hill is fair'.
Turner

SATURDAY 7 FEBRUARY

The nearness of a person or problem pops into my mind disproportionately often.

I forced a 'contemplation' afternoon where, less dramatically than expected, we got to death and *Arandora*. The length of the trauma forced his attention. Reincarnation was mentioned but bungled, he is not ready for it yet. A strong subject occupation facilitates continuous object fixation.

We came to Freud via the fear of expectation and hypochondria rather more than I bargained for. It is a fairly heavy responsibility – even the correct diagnosis won't help much. It seems that in my case, the *Arandora* affair took enough energy for itself to be no longer blind in the face of the other question – not to forget Anita.

I wish I could help him. But there would have been more chance of success if it all had come about naturally, as in Walter's case. Here, to some extent, I've forced things nearer together than they would have come naturally. They would not have done so at all, that is the only excuse, and I cannot deny that so far, I'm the gaining party or one gaining party at any rate and I shall remain it too.

SUNDAY 8 FEBRUARY

It is the small event that is significant now – not the 2 Mozart piano concerts of last night nor even the Bach double concert, but Fred showing his way of cutting my oval birthday cake into ten parts and remarking, in his quiet deepish voice, that of course he did not know it for certain, but he believed that some of the mathematicians of antiquity had solved the 'problem of the cake'.

Uwe turned 26.

Today we were together with a few others – but that's no good, nothing comes out of it really. Going to get *Lord Jim* for him to 'show him a real failure'. At present I am set on Huxley as an introduction to Freud.

Uwe Radok.
Radok family collection.

WEDNESDAY 11 FEBRUARY

Sunday closed on a week of black despair after having heard something about Fred's life and family so far. There seemed to be little to look back to and present worries are not those of the 'luxury variety'. The problem of how to 'insert something positive' is almost impossible, psychoanalysis of course is just a scratch.

Monday we worked together, and spent the evening in his circle. They are all rather convincing specimens and talk very English, Cambridge of course. In the evening there was a 'party' with a few called for and some uncalled-for guests. Maths and physics were discussed, with great influence on Rainer. Interesting enough, but fundamentally on a different star about the task for scientists to preserve themselves for after the war. Generally, in this connection, there is a nervous crisis for scientists out of work in the war and there have been several tragic cases. I am wondering whether Fred's depression is just momentary – I could not compete with so much excellence.

> Among the *Dunera* population was a group of confirmed Anglophiles, many of whom had been educated in England and had lived there for several years before the war. Some insisted on speaking only English, never German, and adopted other affectations in ostentatious displays of learning and privilege.

Tuesday was altogether unsatisfactory. Knowing it is all a matter of destination, what use is there in trying to force things, 'the patient will swerve back in its own time'. Psychological analysis is probably not going to come off, resistance was after all to be expected. Since it cannot profitably be taught anyway but requires more energy to be effective, the hint will prove sufficient in time. All afterthoughts are usually unimportant, compared with the first reality. I resort to looking and enjoying, and wait for times instead of trying to make them myself.

All evening I looked in vain for a certain quotation of topical interest. I found it using the *Bible of the World* notes, the first time this system of diary notes has proved its usefulness, although no easy reference is possible. From the Hindu scripture, 'he who is beloved is still beloved though he acts falsely. To whom is not the body clear, although it be corrupted by all kinds of faults.'

The day started fairly enthusiastically, then I met difficulties in supporting the construction of shelves for Fred, our 'work'. The light gradually failed and in the afternoon he was in a bad mood until we cut it short and had tea together. Once you've found out what somebody likes you are fairly safe, even if it is no longer the ambitious plan of fundamentally changing life for him. In principle, nearness can't be forced but must have time to grow organically – as I should have known. Maybe it will, yet.

The last two weeks have been a good rehearsal – they have shown many defects and a few advances, mainly in the growing disillusionment regarding my capabilities and the value of many things held dear so far.

THURSDAY 12 FEBRUARY

Somehow problems disappeared again and it is more like the first days, just enjoying sight and presence. Having vomited all contents, this shows that I should not do it and that no satisfaction is to be gained by trying to force something which must come about naturally – or not at all. Compare this with the superior man who acts according to what he says and believes – but acts first and maybe talks after. I have dreams but little inclination for analysis, after all what can the result be except what we already know. The situation is bound to produce some symptoms, maybe it will become serious after the war – if there is an after.

Afternoon: 'Now it's old, I'm beginning to doubt my day'. There is a distinct improvement, even one or two relapses of no consequence. I need to try to avoid being conscious of the progress of the affair – after all it has been the right thing in the case of carpentry and is likely to be so generally.

I made a grave mistake of not keeping all this to myself, at least unless I am asked for it, 'vielleicht liebt er an dir den ungebrochen blick der ewigheit'. 'Maybe he loves the unbroken eye and the gaze of eternity about you.'

There is an advantage of being in the wrong, it gives the other an easy chance to show himself as generous. I should confine myself to short occasional walks, if at all. Luckily there is a lot to do and I'm feeling up to it again.

Somehow everything is right today, in spite of the heat. We worked to exhaustion without either part losing temper. Fred in his best light for which I claim some credit without knowing exactly whereby it was brought about. My main fault has been hope not controlled – to communicate myself – shan't happen again.

Letter from parents in America, little cheerful news but comparatively speaking satisfactory. The idea of meeting them again instinctively classed as improbable. If it happens it will be learning to know each other from the beginning.

SATURDAY 14 FEBRUARY

Yesterday, the day was set aside for designing shelves. Later there was a notice from Layton, none for Fred with results known well enough to people in our position. Nevertheless, in the evening, we listened to records after a tremendous thunderstorm with near lightning with colossal shocks, the intensity of the impression as not for a long time. But for the first time in my life there was not the least fear! Everything was all right, when I found some plausible way of getting rid of my last peach.

Today I started work alone and immediately bungled everything by yielding to S's ideas instead of sticking to our own. Afterwards I made a pitiful attempt at braving it out, without success of course. I feel like going to offer to dissolve the partnership in view of my own incapability.

Meanwhile it appears to me that some of it may be due to the crime of feigning interest for something that does not interest me very much. Trying to reach one aim while pretending to pursue another is, psychologically, very likely to lead to failure. If that is so, there exists no way out at present and the only thing to do is to be exceedingly careful. After all, in the Scottish Gliding Union, I was quite capable of a certain degree of leadership, meaning and concentrating just on it.

The rule for the next 'dark shadow': work for myself and don't bother – it will assist him to get out of it.

SUNDAY 15 FEBRUARY

Last night there was a talk on British social work, humanities. Rather similar in being greatly impressed by certain things without being able to produce a great amount of detailed reason in support of it.

There is the difficulty of transferring impressions and feelings, maybe it is a reason for my solitary tendency – dreamer.

Today started badly enough with an argument with Jobst and his reproach of being over nervous in the last 10 days. That was to be expected since the sexual component and underlying force has to be disappointed. It won't last much longer anyway.

Having slight self-reproaches at the neglect of math but I think it's justified. Development is rather like scanning through a telescope and using the adjustment. If there is a jam it may mean that one has to apply force or that one has to turn back and set the focus anew; in the latter case force could damage the whole system.

This does not in any way mean analysis that can be compared to cutting, raising the flesh and skin of a sore! In severe cases this will be necessary, and I have to accept the unpleasantness that is after all real, it always brings out the worst of man. But if there is no real necessity, the process of laying it bare will be harmful and may prevent a natural recovery. For the first time, there is the realisation of the fact that an increase of consciousness does not mean progress in itself, as Jung has it. Freud says with normal sexuality there can be no neuroses.

The period of fruitfulness has almost past now, there remains only a last attempt to help him somewhat with far less presumption than at first. I have felt the difficulties and then my own inadequacy, after the first short period where consciousness could keep things straight. But that period is bound to be short, the vibration subsides and only the forced one remains and shows the true core. Nothing will ever lead anywhere unless it comes about naturally, gradually growing after a peak start, instead of diminishing intensity.

MONDAY 16 FEBRUARY

Bad news from everywhere – Churchill may be out presently. I have an idea for a cartoon – a vehicle or the ship of state going a sharp turn to the left and some people can't turn that way and just fly off by centrifugal force. The turn started rather early; first Chamberlain flew off – he had taken an incline of sorts but not the right one etc.

In the evening there is a long conference on the canteen. Fred is very charming but definitely detached. I realise again that my 'method' was wrong. One must wait. As it is, we are in a kind of deadlock where only a fortunate accident can make any difference. If there isn't one, the balance may just be that, by being rather unusually open and showing more of my defects than absolutely necessary. I have given the other, without wanting it this way consciously, more confidence in himself. This after all was the main purpose at some time.

WEDNESDAY 18 FEBRUARY

I finished that day by reading dream theory deep into the night. Yesterday was fairly hard work. I read Aurelius and found a few points after all, one or two applying to Fred.

The Fred situation lost much of its vexation by realising now that the mistake has been to combine two incompatible things.

THURSDAY 19 FEBRUARY

Yesterday morning I read Freud on inversions, and found it confirmed that an exchange of feeling is quite the rule, and help for the other person a frequent motive, a tableau. After that, a busy and successful day. In the evening there was a musical party with no lapses regarding keeping too near. When leaving, a movement reminded me of the wave from the tram received on a similar occasion. This appears to have constituted a kind of finis since detachment and a more objective view of Fred definitely increased during today, while a few days ago it took an effort to leave him. I continued showing him pertinent extracts from Marcus Aurelius, which after all was quite a lucky hit and in principle can be maintained.

The interest in our own situation is growing, which is a reflection on the Quakers' inadequacy. They knew we were designated A and never said so. We could have been out long ago, it seems.

The Society of Friends, better known as the Quakers, played a prominent role in helping the *Dunera* internees with advice and comforts such as books. In some cases, Quakers were able to facilitate the passage of internees back to Britain. Most *Dunera* men thought fondly of the Quakers and the support they offered, seeing them as a bridge to civil society.

WEDNESDAY 25 FEBRUARY

It is a fact that one feels 'disturbed' when being too near to somebody – a few yards off is all right.

SATURDAY 28 FEBRUARY

The canteen is finished so we could move now. It would be nice to join a few pleasant people but of course I can't wait for that. Besides I am becoming sterile again – I can't force things. Psychological analysis idea is practically dropped – of course it must not suit everybody alike. Some people don't need it because of their pronounced equilibrium, but if one lacks that, it is a valuable help to go on, even without aim or illusion. I know that both will turn up again, sometime. As it is, both 'planes of vision' are frequently disturbing each other. I am reading Freud, it is very complicated, maybe it is possible by repeated condensation of notes to even shorter ones.

SUNDAY 1 MARCH

Reading *Jane Eyre* – it is rather artificial, though behind it there may be enough impulse. In the evening, on hearing from Rainer about Fred's being depressed despite the canteen success, I decide to let him have *Lord Jim* now, after all it is the most sensible thing to do since I don't know how long this life is going to last.

MONDAY 2 MARCH

Poisoned toe and holiday – maths lectures – but it is rather a waste of time. By now it seems rather certain that this subject alone is no longer satisfying. Thus, it would be more advisable to get what I want to know from a book or leave it just now until more congenial moments – if there are any to come. I seem to have grown out of this stage but what is next? Psychological analysis?

TUESDAY 3 MARCH

Last night we had the first math lesson and afterwards a long walk. There was surprising enthusiasm and I only now realise that a natural and fitting continuation of what started with the canteen has arisen. It would do him a lot of good to get through with math, the most dreaded subject of all. There is work enough for 3 months or longer and this time it is altogether congenial. But it does not look likely that we shall have that long…

WEDNESDAY 4 MARCH

I am reading Dostoevsky's *Idiot* and preciously little can be explained as yet, although some parts, especially those relating to his illness and its manifestation, are somewhat clearer now. But what a book!

Fred's impatience in the face of difficulty should be a clue with the reaction quite out of proportion to the cause. I ought to buy the book, it will be enigmatical for a long time to come yet.

WEDNESDAY 11 MARCH

After some hesitation, yesterday I moved to hut 4. The evening was quite as expected, not satisfying, since Fred went off with somebody far more worthy; still this is something to be glad of.

There is a dramatic struggle to persuade myself for the Labour Corps; we of course are out of it. It is difficult to give advice. The only thing undoubtedly in favour is the fact that usually things I did wrong are less of a sting in my memory than things I failed to do.

The Radok brothers' A classifications acted as barriers to their enlistment in the Australian Army.

SUNDAY 15 MARCH

Wednesday night Fred joined the Labour Corps after all. I felt completely helpless since I could not honestly advise him not to, only to postpone joining until we should be able to too, which may never come off. In a way I'm now responsible, having replied to his angry question about what he should do, by saying that sooner or later he would join. I could never much believe in psychological difficulties or anguish; this was just a small taste of it for the first time. It will probably turn out to be right in the long run, although in the following days I was not at all sure whether I should have pushed him into the water. The fact that I want to jump in too is only partly a justification.

Meddling or not meddling, that is now the question. Probably I could describe life as a continuous attempt not to meddle with other people's business except in a few cases and there to do it thoroughly. After some time he won't be interested in real success as much and will subconsciously try to maintain this way of obtaining satisfaction. Together the picture is fairly complete, with sexual repression which also produces doubts. Still, I remember that the practice of daydreaming tends to disappear later, so he should be all right in the end. During the last days the attachment made rapid progress, or at least so it appeared.

He's got 3 faces and 2 voices, the latter depends on whether he is speaking English, schoolboy or German, far older. The faces could be described as con or sin spiritus and thirdly the face of quite a small boy – like in his registration card– completely off guard and relaxed. To see the last can be counted as a great achievement, just as the con spiritus one is in another way.

The last days have been rather hectic with different snack meals and other improvised excuses for being together – since talk won't work always. There are 1001 topics to talk about but only a few important enough to make it worthwhile. One subject I failed to introduce but there is no need for regret since it would not have been much, of course. Or maybe it was an important omission after all? Three attempts at record playing – meanwhile I knew enough of Fred's psychology to arrange the program as he wanted it, which is not that easy to find out. A straight reply is usually sound, while hesitation and then reply should be taken as contrary in most cases.

The first successful record performance was very impressive for me too, probably on account of abstinence during this week. On such occasions, certain themes impress themselves very intensely, Mozart piano concerto G second movement, D minor first movement beginning, whereas on similar occasions they can be heard without the physical consequences. I understood some remark of Walter's about Mozart's peculiarities in small details or unexpected form variations on this occasion. Last night after the concert, the program brought through successfully against several interventions, we went for a walk and I thought of 'memorable things to say', without results of course. Fred mentioned a 7 month period in London with no money and no work and little food. I can't really wonder at his present condition, or if only that it isn't something quite else.

Today he left – probably the dreams of him will go on for some time as every night this week. It's been a serious attachment after all, a luxury I shan't indulge in for some time now. But it was worth having and I'm glad I stuck through it without any compromises to either my poisoned toe or mathematics or whatnot this time. I doubt that there will be a continuation, it would have been too delightful to stay together for the next times. So, the episode is over. Maybe there will be a few letters and if we are extremely lucky, a meeting in a few years when we have forgotten all about it.

I received a letter from Ian who has been sacked as a pilot and is now doing observer work. Somehow I've a knack of associating with this type of functional failure, though they are splendid otherwise – probably it is an account of the fundamental similarity. Still, I don't wish for anything else.

MONDAY 16 MARCH

Hangover as expected – in general the spirit has gone out of the camp. Still, it won't be long until the next change. Remembering suddenly that after all, certain other people are living too at this moment, and once I am able to imagine how, that is very real.

Labour Corps will do him a lot of good in some ways, and unpleasant things might happen here before long.

WEDNESDAY 18 MARCH

Looking for knowledge to endure this 'ghost life's piercing phantom pain'.

The Americans are reported to be here, in which case things may yet take a different course and England transports become possible again. If only I could have asked Fred to wait at least until we joined too, but his remark that he might just as well do it now, was in the way of it. In fact, he wasn't really expecting any reasons against it and should have looked round further for somebody to push him in. The whole thing continues to worry me a lot, after all is it really essential to get into the army? After all it was on advice from me, disregarding his own wishes. The prospect of maybe doing something about it after the war is very fantastic and remote.

I should have got him to wait.

FRIDAY 20 MARCH

Since yesterday, in spite of his photo, I find it impossible to remember what Fred looks like.

Fred's first letter arrives– to somebody else though. Still, he seems to exist. Makes quite a difference.

SUNDAY 22 MARCH

Though everything today will undoubtedly leave me stale, I'm going to write to Fred anyway.

In the evening another surprise – a German performance of the 9th symphony was excellent. On the whole, rather like times before last Monday.

MONDAY 23 MARCH

Interrupted by a talk with K.H. – a Fred inheritance. He is very young and only in a few points aged by the circumstances. He's trying to study medicine which is something good. I could not help to show off a little since I'm not really interested and, unlike the last case, it comes off very easily and there is no problem to talk for a whole evening. I must beware of talking too much in future, though, since this one is not in any way inclined to see it my way and should not do it either. Rather painting bright what there still is in store for him.

K.H. was likely Kurt Henle, a student from Hamburg. He was born on 18 February 1924, making him one of the youngest *Dunera* internees.

Got the double concerto to copy the second movement and some more Russian. As a whole, it was a busy day and quite different from last week's stupor which shows only occasional signs of returning. The chance to meet Fred again is now so desperately small that I had better prepare for a long time of imperfect communications. It would be good too to work out the lesson of it. I had a dream that Fred was returned 'bright eyed'.

I am making slow progress with Russian but for the past three days at last working at it continuously. Plenty of guessing – but in time it will improve no doubt.

The thought of the letter – which may still come today – is sufficient for a 'flutter'. It is a rather strange development after last week's calm down. I wonder when I am going to have it out with myself.

FRIDAY 27 MARCH

I started reading Marcel Proust, 15 volumes. The first impression is amazing in its completeness and familiarity. Another experience to strengthen that feeling of having been round the world and having found nothing behind it. The journey really started well before coming here anyway, although it was not so clear before I met Fred. Maybe my whole 26 years could be seen as a trot around the world registering impressions from the inside without doing anything about it until some shake-up or other brought me to realise that, essentially, I had got around it and in fact covered some of it twice. Then after some legitimate hesitation I start inside. After all, it may turn out to have been worthwhile, the luxury of delaying this necessary event. Of course, it would have been disappointing to finish still on the outside and without knowing why. I went a bit of the way with Fred and tried my best to pull him inside. Rightly or wrongly, he is in it now.

SATURDAY 28 MARCH

There is the growing feeling that we are not going to get out in time, almost three weeks has passed again without result. I try another letter to Layton, maybe Australians don't want to let us out any longer. It would be just the thing we should expect. Still, it's no good talking about it and Jobst is quite right in getting annoyed.

Again no letter.

Uwe was likely referring to the possibility of the Radok brothers joining the Australian Army. The 8th Employment Company, mooted by Frank Forde in January, came into existence on 7 April 1942. Not until 21 April did the Radoks receive permission to join up. By that time several hundred former *Dunera* internees were already in khaki. A Home Office cable sent to Major Layton on 21 April 1942 stated: 'Radok Brothers … interned because doubtful whether entirely pro-British. Birkett Committee recommended release only if subjected to discipline and effective control. Secretary of State … authorises release for Australian Forces if (repeat if) Australian authorities satisfied on Camp record.' Source: NAA, A2908, P22 Part 8, Internees ex 'Dunera'.

SUNDAY 29 MARCH

I have made good progress with the Fred notes, there is a lot more left open in it than I realised at first, but as a skeleton it is admirable and can be furnished with details later. I realised for the first time the meaning of hypercathexis. It is the difference between looking at a landscape and fixating at a certain point in it which will eliminate the rest.

I realised that the hyper-childish behaviour by some of the young people here is probably just their way of 'symptom formation'. Of course, Fred is rather different and without this way of escape. He is an 'adventurer in theory, conservative at heart' with a rather sombre life in all. There is the exquisiteness of spells of very young mirth or very grownup brilliant word fencing in contrast to the sombre rule.

State of wretchedness.

WEDNESDAY 1 APRIL

The evening before was very like those in Camp 2 when I could not see a single day ahead with any interest. For the first time I caught myself wondering why there is no letter – now that the expectancy is growing less. This was my chance, and I always knew it would be an episode and limited, just as I know that my letter won't come and said that a week ago in a letter to him. This of course does not affect wishes and their disappointment to dominate my feelings.

Tatura at night, by Kurt Winkler. In common with the Radok brothers, Winkler disembarked at Port Melbourne and was taken directly to Tatura. His internment art includes many night scenes. This picture was completed in 1944.
Stocky family collection.

THURSDAY 2 APRIL

I submit to being called a neurotic. I belong to that splendid and pitiable family which is the salt of the earth. All the greatest things we know have come to us from neurotics. Never will the world be conscious of how much it owes to us, nor, above all, what we have suffered in order to bestow their gifts on it.

All not very convincing or I'm not in a mood to like anything.

SATURDAY 4 APRIL

Dream as usual – triumph at being able to see his face. Figuring that we may get out one of these days, training starts next week, but rationally, grave doubts whether anything at all will come of it. Habit of going on walks to get warm getting put into use again.

THURSDAY 9 APRIL

Very empty, only the news that all the fruit pickers have gone into a camp which is almost half a postcard. Made an abortive attempt to hear a string quartet followed by a personal invitation to optics. I was not too keen on it and thus had no difficulty in grasping the principle. Ending in contemplations about pure maths and a long walk in the night.

SATURDAY 11 APRIL

Last night there was a revival in my mood by acting as substitute 2nd violin with a good instrument – a delight. It's probably better to keep the violin up since everything is in order for that still, while by the time the war is over my piano technique won't be superior any longer.

I'm rather disinclined to do anything at the moment. Somehow I have stopped production and gone on to some emergency or depression schedule with a skeleton staff only.

THURSDAY 23 APRIL

Two days ago I started having doubts at my own nihilism. At the same time there was a natural and genuine realisation that if 'the' letter should come, it would hardly stop anything. It is my own problem for which other persons cannot be made responsible seeing that the scale of time is no different inside and outside the barbed wire.

Yesterday I went out with a work party – it's no good waiting for mail.

FRIDAY 24 APRIL

I am no longer waiting for the Home Office reply as now it does not matter when it will come.

MONDAY 27 APRIL

I read another book by Steinbeck – *Of Mice and Men*. Very good and almost inimitable; reminding me of a play, in its simplicity of means. Of course, the impression is probably determined by the 'social complex' which shows more reality than I should have given it credit for.

TUESDAY 28 APRIL

No future is imaginable, thus internment is more or less expected. The other options are only in the future.

SATURDAY 2 MAY

The letter was finished under difficult conditions. The finished product shows painfully clear defects. There is a contrast between density while writing and bareness when just being read, like painting a fresco of which one can't get the right impression before it is finished because one is necessarily too near, or playing a big organ where one ought to have somebody listening far off to direct the registering.

After the letter went away, I saw two of Fred's postcards had just arrived, which unexpectedly gives food for thought. One to H.N. which was very complicated and half apologising for having taken the step and not yet realising that or whether it was a mistake. The other to an Italian which was almost entirely matter of fact and unproblematical. My letter lay in between these two extremes, nearer the realistic one. First thought was depression at having made myself cheaper than I should have and thus forfeiting the best.

H.N. may refer to Heinrich (Henry) Nowottny (1912–2001), a student from Kraschen in Germany.

MONDAY 4 MAY

There is no energy for much more, it seems to belong to an age by now outlived, just as day dreaming has become no longer feasible.

TUESDAY 5 MAY

I wrote a letter to Fred to ask him to look up a few essays about Kropotkin's architectural theory – maybe it does him some good too.

FRIDAY 8 MAY

There is a period of emotion in the camp. These people have belonged to a class that on the whole got a fair deal for so long, that they will never be able to realise that this is not so much a law of nature. Coming from the working class would be an advantage here or at least being able to figure it out approximately. Russell *On Education* is very good but frequently inconsistent as a result of the author's pacifist views with wishful thinking, refusing to realise that instead of making a better material world by his proposed education, it will be necessary to make the material foundation first.

SUNDAY 10 MAY

Release for Labour Corps.

TUESDAY 12 MAY

Going tomorrow – interest lagging.

MELBOURNE, 1942

The evening before leaving camp, I have a long talk with Nowottny who, for the first time showed a little of what he is doing – anthropological methods applied to the analysis of people like the Australians, based partly on books and partly on what he 'feels' of it through the fence. I mentioned Fred and he made the astonishing remark that in his opinion, Fred was one of those who are 'too good for studying', who don't need it, but need only to live.

We left Camp 2 and got to the Caulfield camp which was more equipped. Everything was a big rush, and one could not spare time for wondering. I saw Fred very briefly and was reminded of my first impression.

Yesterday I was still in the camp, bludging with success until the evening. I waited for Fred who came back late and depressed after a rotten job and by the usual miniature difficulties. I went out to dinner with him and partly solved one difficulty by a phoning scheme. Nothing

The 8th Employment Company was stationed first at the Caulfield racecourse. Later it would be based at Camp Pell in Royal Park, and in Broadmeadows on Melbourne's northern fringe.

much has changed and what little analysis there has been does not make any difference. He 'is very pathetic' in his desperate attempts looking for people, a nice girl, while ostentatiously forgetting all about the labour life. I made the usual mistakes such as maintaining that I, at any rate, would not be looking for <u>nice</u> girls without of course either being able, nor thanks god willing, 'to explain' that. I am no longer fooled by this kind of double speak which cannot be successful. Going home we failed to find the name of the camp in the station signboards, and we had to look for it repeatedly. He had a haunted look when getting nearer.

Emil Wittenberg, a former *Dunera* internee and a member of the 8th Employment Company, designed this coat of arms for the unit.
Reproduced with the permission of Martin Burman.

SATURDAY 16 MAY

Last night, after finishing the notes, I went out and tempted every passer in the dark by whistling the second subject of the D minor concerto – and lo! The second one fell for it, and it was Fred. This morning I talked to Goldschmidt who regretted not having been able to live up to his promise of looking after Fred. He was quite frank about its main reason, their fundamentally different dispositions. Thus, Fred came to be friendly with others, mainly two students of philosophy. Both are very nice but that's about all there is to it. No magic in them. Goldschmidt mentioned a decline of bitterness since our arrival, I don't know.

Erich Goldschmidt (1923–1974) was a student from Klein Glienicke in Germany.

We went to a concert in the town hall. Coming late we had to remain in the stalls. Jobst in the beginning was incredibly impressed, for the first time really aware of being free. Afterwards I saw Fred coming out with a rather forbidding looking girl but he did not think so, and looked radiant in a way I have never seen before. If I only could get him to someone worth it; as it is, he must be pretending to himself a good deal and all the charm is utterly wasted on somebody probably far keener on 'movie types'.

TUESDAY 19 MAY

Sunday, two days ago, I went with Fred to the beach. It was no great success, a few lights. Going back, we could not decide about food and went to town. I soundly cursed myself for not remembering Goldschmidt's description of the first night at Kyneton. Here it is almost pathological, in the camp it was not so noticeable. In the evening Loewe told me that he had applied for me as an assistant for

German-born Fritz Loewe (1895–1974), meteorologist and polar explorer, emigrated to Australia in 1937, establishing the Meteorology Department at the University of Melbourne in 1939. He offered practical and emotional support to Uwe and other former internees. During the war he helped to train Royal Australian Air Force navigators.

research on measurement of thermals. The one time there is a probable chance of it coming off.

Yesterday Fred went on the sick list, today he disappeared altogether; but what for I wonder? Last night I spent with Walter and burgundy; got too talkative but it was good to let off steam.

Today I felt rather depressed in spite of my leave. It is obvious that Fred's mirth with the other two is ad hoc and unreal, and that at the bottom of it is the temper I know. But of course it may be also the 'patient swerving back'.

Today I bought *Gösta Berling's Saga* and a murder anthology.

THURSDAY 21 MAY

Yesterday I felt very doubtful about everything, observing the ease at which Fred is with others and how he manifestly enjoys it, while being contrary when he is with me. We went out to work together and I got into a talk with B who is a student of philosophy and proud of it. He is very nice and probably very capable, just a trace too talkative perhaps. It seemed to annoy Fred in a way, he tried to get in a word without succeeding. But the work together was all right, he does more than his fair share and sometimes takes on more than he is able to stand. Returning in the truck, I had a good look at him and did not like the result at all; he's become very nervous, twitching his face when absent minded, which is often. He is always in a hurry to get away, probably rarely with time enough to eat. At any rate he'll find it hard to carry on in the long run.

Working together was all right and even pleasurable – so I'm going to continue aiming at it. I will get him some food during the day and offer similar little help that can be given without making myself a nuisance.

I wonder whether his imitative tendency to assimilate himself to his surroundings and to make a special effort at that would explain some of the facts that puzzled me yesterday. Of course the difficulty is that I do not know.

In two days I will start working at meteorology, the other thing that matters just now.

Lazy day in all.

Fred is in the next hut and unreachable. I'm crazy to brood like that without taking the trouble to realise that it is all a 'ghost life's piercing fantastic pain'. But what does it all mean, what are we going to do! All the quotations say it: 'to bow and accept the end', 'in sleep a king, but in waking no such matter, really are we sleeping before and are awake now'.

Bloody, bloody, bloody.

FRIDAY 22 MAY

In this spirit I went to town. I caught an express train by mistake and thus conveniently got rid of all my plans, only to be accosted by Fred on the street. We had tea together and it was quite harmonious except that, for the first time, I said all the things I had in mind not to say. This is no advice from Confucius. I spoilt the end for myself at least, by an incapability to leave him at the right moment, but on the whole I liked it and it probably was good to tell him about his twitching.

Tonight we had dinner together and all went very well indeed. He must have really liked it because he did not offer any thanks but just said so.

Day work without the personal background, rather dreary. I almost had to miss the appointment when we started loading at 3.30 in the afternoon. In my own case this may be the only possibility to get something out of this sort of life.

But it is not good if one is either not built that way or does not meet a person, the mere presence of whom is sufficient to make everything all right.

MONDAY 25 MAY

On Saturday I answered roll call for Fred who only turned up again on Sunday morning. Work without him is rather bleak; it is dangerous to get so dependent on it, but there the matter lies.

The philosophers at work are rather amusing, especially the one who reminded me strongly of Fred in his way of talking. I later found out that they lived together for more than a year.

Sunday I went to town with Fred but had to leave him when all his plans failed to come off and I went to see Loewe, which was wholly enjoyable.

Today again we worked together. I spent moments wondering about the whole infatuation. However, I only need to think of internment to accept everything gladly with tiredness. In the evening, I had a hasty dinner with Walter and Fred and too much port and afterwards a rehearsal at the conservatorium. Fred was very much impressed, it was successful and one of those things I hoped to manage. A nice girl of course would be even better.

We talked about Burger whom I like for his calm seriousness while Fred finds him changed since the fruit picking and prone to only fool around and does not like it, while always aiding his part in it.

THURSDAY 28 MAY

I saw the library for the first time, another sign of freedom. It's difficult to get past the initial step of just looking around though, so a more or less wasted evening as far as results are concerned. Work day with Fred and mixed feelings. He went away impatiently and down at lunchtime to try and buy Graves' *Claudius* in Penguin. I happened to pick it up, but this time the surprise was spoiled by his finding a copy himself. I managed, with some effort, to keep my enterprise concealed, although it would have been difficult to say why I thought it advisable.

I went to have a look at flats in the evening, saw one very good building.

After the library, I had a talk with Walter who is still at the cross-roads. Another responsibility, this time a real one, not forced.

Today Fred scrammed and I felt somewhat uneasy all morning wondering whether it was maybe just funk that prevented me from doing the same. More probably it's the lack of definite aims. What to do with the time?

There are plenty of possibilities, but none of them is so essentially different from shifting boxes. It seems I really do not care much for anything any longer, in spite of being wretched or very happy at times. It is all sham and I just drag on without intensity.

Tonight I tried to read Brunt's *Meteorology* and fell asleep. After that I tried a strange poem-play by Edna St Millay and that worked better. Maybe I'll have to confine myself to looking things up when required as studying does not seem to have become any more feasible. At times I feel satisfaction at a working-class existence. That interest is about the only one left.

SATURDAY 30 MAY

Yesterday, after good work and mood in the canning factory, everything went wrong in the evening. The rehearsal was disappointing, as Walter remarked surprisingly: one should not try the same joys twice in short succession, and we went home, silent all the way. I came to the conclusion that the initial period of excitement had passed and now I am unable to ignite Fred's spirits. In that case, I should avoid contact, except during work and if anything at all, try to make him help himself rather than interfere. Today we nearly got separated at parade but a mistake in counting made everything all right. There was no talk during the evening except a few words on Graves' *Claudius*, reading it at the same time, a new 'vice'. One of his remarks was highly illuminating and in one confirmed my psychological speculations in a certain direction regarding our similarity. He was talking of the cruelties and vice, perversion, 'but he never gives any details, that is the pity'. This gives a new importance to the idea which Walter probably could bring off.

Coming home, we found new regulations regarding leave. By chance I got Fred's pass and he was grateful, before he asked for me at the tent for the first time – 'what a thrill'! We went out together and I had the opportunity to hint at math and to see he was not disinclined – at least at the time. It confirmed another of my conjectures by saying that when absent without leave he felt hunted all the time and did not enjoy that part of it. Maybe dinner would have been a fiasco too, but for two RAAF men on our table. Afterwards we listened to Friedmann's *Variations Sérieuses* by Mendelssohn which were quite good, as well as Chopin *Préludes*. The last, D minor of Peter fame, happened to be the one that impressed Fred most too and I like the coincidences. Coming home, I felt rather tired again but I'm not so sure whether that is altogether bad. The fooling around would not be very genuine in my case and as a rule sounds hollow. Maybe I'm too old and perhaps that explains being less at ease. Still the verdict of last night will have to stand, after all I will have to use my evenings for myself some of these days.

Full moon – everything very light and the tent camp really beautiful.

MONDAY 1 JUNE

Yesterday I stayed in the camp as the first experiment, dodging the process of being noted down on the reserves list. I went to town alone in the evening after B had made a few very cute remarks about Fred, proving that he realises the problem too, although he is not personally interested. I am feeling very low which is the penalty for forgetting about everything else of course, for living for the one thing only. Same today at work – although it passed rather quickly.

Last night visit to Alsens and arranged for a private piano recital. Cologne had a very heavy raid, this is the beginning of the war as utopistic authors saw it and quite possibly there won't be much left in Europe after it is finished.

MONDAY 8 JUNE

Changing moods, but on the whole there is less intensity. I'm living on a drug just now. There can be no doubt after the experience of being separated by my own inexcusable behaviour, in spite of almost 4 weeks army life in the open.

Bayer's ideas about Fred are just the same, only I don't think his remedy would meet the case and I ought to be able to judge this particular case.

Mrs Alsen – we escaped something when we missed the piano recital last week – but she is very nice and apparently been known to show up since I abandoned the idea. She's very young in many respects and it's a pity she's got that husband. A typical marriage it seems.

Piano is beginning to appeal again. Having managed to forget all my exhibition pieces but one, I must be careful to keep away from them in future and concentrate on Bach.

I met one of Lebrecht's people, hope there will be more. That at least is a society which holds some prospects, not those people one seems to have outgrown, together with the feeling of hours in bourgeois comfort and uneasiness in a dark, dreary sub-station. Those who I have outgrown have swapped their reality values.

So far so good – but there remains something to be done before anything complete can be attempted.

Today magnificent – no work, sleep in the sun, constantly dreaming of the drug.

Dr Franz Lebrecht, born in Mainz in 1901, was an economist. In 1934 he was arrested by the Gestapo while placing red roses on the grave of Rosa Luxemburg on the anniversary of her birthday. He spent four years in Nazi concentration camps as a political prisoner. He was deported from Singapore to Australia on the *Queen Mary* in 1940, and was interned at Tatura until January 1942. He died in Berlin in the late 1970s. When exactly is not known.

WEDNESDAY 10 JUNE

Two days with the dope, the slang term is so much better, making it abundantly clear that some change is about to take place and that under the present conditions nothing else can be expected. What is required is the capability of infusing spirit and obviously it is missing. This again shows that it represents <u>my</u> own problems and that the object is incidental – though accidentally worthwhile.

Yesterday I made an abortive attempt to get a step further with Walter which was postponed for the lack of vital information. Of course, the proper way would be waiting for the real opportunity, and I can imagine what it would be like. But there is neither the time nor any inclination for that and there remains only the less artistic alternative besides, of course, postponement. However, I can rule that out.

There is already more in the way of subjects than there will be time to do them.

Library work is rather handicapped by my continuously dozing off although no longer with such obvious dreams as one night two weeks ago. Tonight raises some hope that at some time stability may be reached, irrespective of what may happen in the way of changes.

The dope problem will probably find its solution surprisingly soon after I become normal. In a way it will be a pity 'to bow and accept the end', the end of the spell, that started when first noticing him. He mentioned yesterday that he thought me the youngest then and that 'it was a compliment' – without explaining why. But maybe we will become friends after all, that would make up for it.

Today for no manifest reason I felt curiously elated. For the first time I honestly enjoyed solitariness.

SATURDAY 13 JUNE

Thursday I scrammed with the dope and went to Upper Ferntree Gully. Everything was perfect, starting with an improvised breakfast and ending with catching the right bus after having found the way through the thick of a forest. In the evening we had records at Pat's, another successful 'improvisation'. His finishing remark, a rare thing nowadays: 'it was a good day'. Personally speaking, there have been working days I enjoyed just as much; mere landscapes somehow do not seem to suffice any longer.

Yesterday I was on leave – breakfast at Alsens and after that, tennis. I played my own style and of course I easily despair at not finding myself a Wimbledon champion at the first attempt.

I gave 'a few useless bits of advice' and left, not easily, but far more so than even a short time ago. The superior line is perhaps the only one, 'perhaps he loves you with the unbroken gaze of eternity'. After all previous experience, this one or two days of concentrated perfection is very exhausting and the result is to consolidate everything that seemed puzzling and unstable before. Why I could not say. Something of fundamental importance must have happened but all I know is that it started with that one evening; how?

Uwe mentions Pat regularly. Almost certainly this was Pat Gray (1920–2020), who was part of an intellectual and artistic circle of Melburnians who befriended various *Dunera* boys. Pat, later known as Ailsa Fabian, taught history at the University of Melbourne. In about 1943 she joined the Australian Army's Directorate of Research and Civil Affairs. After the war she became a noted author. Gray married the artist Erwin Fabian, a former *Dunera* internee. Photograph: Pat Gray, circa 1955. Courtesy of Mark McKenna and Ailsa Fabian.

MONDAY 15 JUNE

Yesterday, after a remark about night classes, I 'tripped the catch' and out came the same contemplations of old, with a period of intensive inferiority feelings which can't be eliminated by rational refutation. He's afraid of work, in short, all the symptoms we know so well. However, the background is very different. He had uninspiring parents, no attachment that would lead to 'repetition compulsion'. He never cared too greatly for anybody it seems and probably vice versa seeing the helloffa lot of energy it takes not to lose contact.

We went to a dance together, not much of a success in my case but as a whole worthwhile, another missing link. Taste – not too bad. New is an active attachment on his part since the AWL day – I think we are beyond the worst now. There is a kind of transference in a narcissistic case, something for Freud. But the result may be worthwhile.

Today we worked together. Philosophy, rather annoying in the longer run, I'm afraid. Got in a poem discovered yesterday, MacNeice *Autumn VI*. In the evening there was general undecidedness as to what to do and I ended up alone with Walter in the Dugout to hear an American band. I could not stand it long for heat and noise and went to sit in the hall where I saw a girl I had noticed before without realising why. I made visible progress in talking to her and ensuring continuation. Of all things.

The Dugout, opened in 1942, was a Norman Myer initiative for servicemen and women. Two cafes were joined together beneath the Capitol Theatre in Swanston Street, Melbourne, providing food and entertainment, bathrooms, and a clothes-mending room. The Dugout was staffed by 150 volunteers from Myer's department store.

Dancers at the Dugout, 1942.
National Library of Australia, PIC P805/1673 LOC Album 1139.

TUESDAY 16 JUNE

Today coming home from the library I met Fred. Yesterday he lost his watch and today he forgot his pipe, fountain pen and a started letter at some place where he did not intend to go again for some time. He was despairing of everything, including his mental capacities in making conversation. He proposed to consult me as psychologist some day, the deadlock does not seem to loosen in his case. 'Day dreaming all the time, beating up people, things one could not tell'. Smoking in the dark lighting up his face from time to time, symbolic of the whole affair.

It becomes a responsibility; he must not be let down. Maybe the influence of some complete person would have been better but then as a rule they just don't trouble. As long as I can get him to the edge of the bag, the transferences will solve themselves easily when he gets eyes to see.

At present there is a growing attachment, in places even too intensive perhaps, but now is not the time for drawing back.

Today we also moved to another camp with the usual wearying details. I tried in vain to get into the same tent as Fred. These endeavours mainly failed by his indecisiveness to leave his present, not altogether convincing, group. I forgot or failed to 'prepare the ground' for the one really good group in the camp.

I was feeling rotten over it in the evening while nothing was settled as to our own problem. For the first time Fred seems aware of another's feelings and is very nice about it, saying 'don't feel bloody, promise me', before going out. A typical case of gaining in comparison from somebody's lack of it. In this connection, the question arises whether my own 'superiority' of the last days was created at his cost. However, so far there is no real proof for the truth of that suspicion. Probably it is rather a case of releasing bound and ill balanced energies for which no great influence is required.

The 8th Employment Company moved from Caulfield racecourse to Camp Pell in Royal Park, just north of Melbourne's business district.

THURSDAY 18 JUNE

We were separated on parade, but I was affected less keenly. I should like to know what kind of day it was for Fred. But it won't be possible to find out. In fact, I'm talking too much and it is giving things away to H that nobody ought to know.

There are bad prospects for the problem of living in the same tent.

SATURDAY 20 JUNE

Two days ago Fred got very sick on drink and seems to have given away a lot. Still, it is fairly safe. There is a drought in our relations again. The 'new item' is telling me off which at least shows some interest. Even so, I'm beginning to wish I could hand my 'commission' back completed. The subjective part has lasted long enough and is beginning to be a nuisance at times. H and J are making faces at each other about Fred's company at work. The objective part of course is almost as far from completion as can be, even if the analysis has been completed. Thus, waiting for the right moment now.

Evening spent in the library – too tired to do anything.

TUESDAY 23 JUNE

Sunday I nearly scrammed but then we got off at lunch without scramming. We went to play tennis, there was a slight improvement on both sides. Once the 'untidiness' has been eliminated he ought to have no difficulties. The rule of prohibiting curses and apologies is useful again.

Monday was spent on leave. I had a talk to Mrs Alsen. It's a pity she did not marry somebody else, she gives the impression of having come off her own track to a state beyond repair. But that may be only on the face of it. I will try to find out tomorrow when going to the theatre although I should prefer falling ill and sending Fred to take my place. Yesterday I got him invited much against his will and my own liking at first. However, a walk was arranged for him by asking Rainer to take over Mr Alsen, and later Fred had a talk with the two little girls, all of which went to save the evening. He enjoys talking to girls aged 12, of course it is easy. If only I could.

WEDNESDAY 24 JUNE

Yesterday after lunch, no work but sleep for two hours.

It was a perfect evening here in camp. Afterwards I went to a Chinese restaurant with H where we were met by Fred and a man called Nicholson. We went to a lecture on political science. The lecturer was very impressive, a closer look will be possible next Sunday. Fred was struggling hard to keep awake and making faces all the time. Afterwards we had some records at N's place and continuous 'brilliant conversation' which some time back would have made me feel very inferior.

Today Fred was on leave again for 'special preparation'. By now the effect is different and the absence is not very important or rather his presence would not make much of a difference. It looks like the beginning of emancipation, leaving only the objective problem. The solution is as far away as ever. I plan to fall sick and send him to the theatre, unless he is still or again in camp. But it is not a wholly satisfactory scheme and thank God does not depend on this one detail. M took the hint marvellously and talked to him whenever possible, for example on our walk when I managed to neutralise Rainer against the husband.

SATURDAY 27 JUNE

The theatre was disappointing, and I was lucky that the plan did not come off, also because of Mrs Alsen's behaviour. It was admittedly necessitated by the circumstances, but I don't know whether she could not act the 'bright young thing', which she may be of course. The marriage probably spoiled her too much, unless somebody comes along who is older and very much more interested. But there it is the same problem as with Fred, it would be lucky to the extreme if somebody did. Thursday was a long job. Fred went to Alsens' friends and did not like it – good!

Yesterday Fred took me to task for a facetious remark made to somebody in a camp washroom talking German at the top of his voice, and a few other 'complaints' came out as well. Somehow this is a great step forward since the time when I could only get at him by a frontal attack, a method which of course still yields the best results.

The appointment last night did not come off and instead I met the editor of a soldiers' educational magazine, who may turn out to be quite worthwhile.

SALT (1941–1946) was an educational magazine published by the Australian Army for its soldiers. The name of its editor is not known. Editions of the magazine identify individual authors, but not the editor.

I talked to Major Layton in the evening. I was unnecessarily rude, as usual, although I had no known intention of the kind. My prospect of becoming a driver for the Americans was not exactly helped.

This morning Fred scrammed alone while I missed my turn. I have an aversion to scramming after the party has been put together on dirty days like this one, since it means that the others have to work harder.

It turned out to be a perfect day, and one practically without work. I felt like a deserter in view of the promise to go with him whenever he wanted. Personal inadequacy is becoming more intensive every day. It seems I shall be my bright old same self again if it goes on like this. I am feeling dissatisfied, nihilistic and above all losing power over my talk, especially to people I dislike. I must try to do something about that.

Of course, that is rot. The evening in camp was quite enjoyable after all, especially the walk back in the moonlight. Probably a lack of sleep is all that is wrong. I am no longer manifestly tired but increasingly unable of coordinating action and intention and speech. For example, I was terribly rude, in a confused way, to A about answering his name on roll call and I forgot to fetch Fred's leave pass.

I've got out of bed again to write the possible explanation. Living in an artificial, intellectually-made balance instead of a natural equilibrium of forces, and control suffers as soon as a certain degree of tiredness has been reached. It reminds me that there is still the problem to be solved, the dissatisfaction about which state of affairs certainly plays a part.

MONDAY 29 JUNE

Yesterday the log out of the church parade was a wash out. Fred was sulking as hardly ever before, but after some time got out by himself. There are plenty of ways to affect this, but the natural end is the best. I mentioned his Matric, obtained unexpectedly and in opposition to the whole of the school authorities. I got him on to ping-pong – a new bait for emergencies, besides he beats me hollow.

In the afternoon was trench digging in the sun and the reaction I hoped for. He manages to enjoy these things which is a great advantage over those who are purely intellectual. We scrammed and went to the South Yarra club for squash which was a great success and must be repeated. Physical exercise of that sort is certainly among the most positive things you can do for him just now. With regard to other things, there may be better people; for example, Mr N whom he stayed with on Saturday. On my remark that he had a better time there than he would have had, had I scrammed too, there came a denial of this truth but not a very convincing one. After all, my objection is limited to the special complex of problems I'm in a position to judge better than any of his friends, and it would be foolish to aspire much further in view of my own well-known inadequacies in general.

In the evening Paul and listening to Op 127– the first visit to people I really enjoyed. Hope there will be more.

Today I had lunch with Fred in the camp, then ping-pong, very harmonious and stable, quite unreal. Afterwards I could not get going and had a grey afternoon, in spite of the sunshine and work in the open air on grass. I felt fagged and gloomy and dog tired for no particular reason. But it is a waste of time I may regret some day.

After that I went to hear Walter's new arrangement, touching in its difficulty to comprehend, even here – but klavier fur volk and Fred coming home late – enjoying the moment.

TUESDAY 30 JUNE

We worked together – had a long and rather superfluous discussion with H about Plato as 'fascist' with Fred in the 'chair'. Good ideas on his part – very serious, H is not easily taken in or swept aside by irrational motives. It was a perfect setting for a play, on stacks of boxes and some soldier butting in with his opinion on politics.

Later I got Fred on to math. Perhaps we can start a course. Catering for amusements is too tiring and unsatisfactory in the long run. The world is definitely going to bits but it's no use taking that into consideration here. When going out he asked somebody else whether he was still going to the college and got as a reply '4 nights a week, but of course it's for myself', and with that motto I shoved him off to the tech but probably he didn't go.

Tomorrow we shall scram and play tennis, I hope.

WEDNESDAY 1 JULY

Scrammed in the morning – beautiful realisation of freedom, even if it is illegal. Tennis was rather a washout, largely due to my rotten form. Lunch was a success and afterwards I managed to make him take a 'snooze'. Perfect peace – if only it was permanent and post-war. I committed to memory the last movement of no.1 Partita, I must try and play the no.2. Later there was more tennis which was a complete wash out and almost certainly my fault. I could not concentrate, either for bodily or mental disturbances. So, we dropped it and immediately there was a state of satisfaction again.

In the evening Jobst dropped in. He is a magnificent specimen, thriving on every side, writing a two-page letter in 10 minutes and showing promise of becoming an excellent welder, fixing up our money affairs etc. Seeing him, one is tempted to think everything more subtle is somewhat artificial and superfluous, but that fallacy is easily destroyed. Still a bit more of that type would not do any harm to anybody.

Home early, in a warm springlike storm. It was not a bad day but very different from the intense excitement of the first time. Everything is getting more solid and natural, and I almost believe Fred would remember me if we could get to different places, even though the main problem remains unsolved.

THURSDAY 2 JULY

Libia is looking worse than ever. There is debate in the Commons regarding the equipment side. Lyttelton says our weapons should be better than the enemy's, but there are difficulties about that central principle. Democratic countries who wanted peace found that when war came, we could not afford to interrupt the production of weapons which were serviceable but inferior to those of the enemy. We were at a great disadvantage against an enemy whose weapons were equal to all his immediate needs.

I finished the *New Statesman* without even dropping off for a single time. A remarkable achievement, especially under the circumstances where the way to studies of any kind appears to be blocked by the same old trouble and a few new considerations.

Never before have I felt the first so clearly.

Afterwards I tried Robert Frost with no success. Then I hit at something better, *Fleurs du Mal*. Again, there is a problem, the inescapability of which, in literature at any rate, used to puzzle me: realising very clearly that we have been building a superstructure without foundations and that hardly any more can be added before this is corrected. Tonight that seems very easy and it is going to be so. Picking somebody off the street has become quite natural – I wonder what next.

SUNDAY 5 JULY

An evening with Walter. I missed a good chance, and he took me to a dance which was a wash out. He falls under the category too, in spite of the different sexual basis, which is an argument against Freud or a proof of the statement that not just any way of sexual activity solves the problem.

Yesterday I went on leave with Fred who left me in the morning and wasn't seen again, just heard on the phone. The job of entertainer to His Majesty is becoming rather tedious. I should be grateful to others for taking over this function as has happened already to a large extent.

Today we scrammed again, after a worried night about how to manage Fred's absences in the morning. It's no longer very enjoyable after I have seen that it works and begin to think more frequently of other implications. The group really is the main argument. The rest of the crowd would not matter so much; but I want to keep together with them after all, or at least Fred does and ought to.

The day was wasted. I ought to have gone gliding instead of just laying on the couch and staring at clouds passing by.

TUESDAY 7 JULY

I didn't enjoy Sunday in any way until we hit on a volume of Bach's Organ for 4 Hands – a magnificent passacaglia which I hope will be practised. We went to squash in the afternoon. Fred was very cramped again and helplessly furious, so my advice was not much good. I had a good game with Jobst who was 'pleasantly disappointed', which of course represents a great success.

Afterwards I went to a Jewish dance in a state of caring for nothing in particular. Fred proffering his lack of skill in contacting.

Today there was hard work outside and a weak attempt at maths. A fight at the mess hut engrossed Fred's imagination with him scheming about what he would have done. He said that a girl was the thing that mattered most for him just now. Whether that is merely an echo I don't know.

I took him to task for not going to the architect studies club and for a ridiculous lack of self-esteem, unnecessary even under his condition and also for spoiling all new acquaintances right in the beginning by apologeticness.

Actually a club of that sort would rapidly solve the problem if he is lucky, a common interest makes a very good start.

Last night I had dreams again, very frank in representing Fred as the double figure but in waking life things have changed and we are nearer a state of friendship than ever before. His momentary absence is no longer a disturbance; criticism more awake.

WEDNESDAY 8 JULY

Walter discovered 'a place' so things may come to a pass now at last. It will be a nice birthday present if it is found to be satisfactory.

I had an unpleasant experience of slipping in the truck and knocking my head on the sideboard. I acted stunned for the spectators' benefit only – alone there would have been nothing of the sort.

FRIDAY 10 JULY

Yesterday again only Fred and Stephen. Stephen is very nice but with no madness about him. In the evening there was a party at S's – not very exciting. Fred has been 'in good temper for the last three days', of course only as long as he is together with people he knows. Once he gets rid of that 'restriction' I would agree completely with Walter that he would be a tremendous hit with the girls. As it is, the ice has to be broken first. I remember that I used to be the same, or still am?

Coming home at two o'clock completely awake and quite serene in spite of the complete lack of any good reasons for it, unless one considers the decision on such an important matter as what to buy Fred as a birthday present. Of course, there may be more behind it on the more definite prospect of getting a step further.

This morning we got split up. First of all St was on leave, then the group failed to fall in at the end, which as it turned out would not have made any difference, then I was cut off from the rest and put into the next and last big party. If I had been Fred, I should have gone into the big party too. Well, he didn't. We went out in the same truck, and he seemed to have forgotten my presence, so I did not bother to look his way when they left us. No ill feeling, only it has been brought home to me again that there is still an incongruity left. It would be natural if either side wanted a change, but this is somewhat different. Well, there the matter rests. I don't think there will be anything to come of it. Most likely he did not notice me at all, although I wonder.

Nothing came of it.

MONDAY 14 JULY

Saturday we built tents including our own. Until that had been accomplished, there was a tense situation with rudeness all round including myself v Fred and wrongly so. In cases where I'm interested, I still have as little power of keeping my temper. Birthday party was in the evening. The dinner was magnificent, after that rather a decline and fall, except the dancing which was enjoyable at times. Rainer was in top form with a rather petrified girl who, however, seemed to gain life as a result of his attentions. Maybe he's got the knack, at any rate no need to worry about him.

I got home at 4 and loaded 285 tons the next day. Fred was very down in the morning so that even Stephen mentioned it and started pricking him up on my instigation. That made him liven up again for nearly the whole working time.

We went to play squash without major illusions as to what it would be like and had a really good game. Yesterday was drill and a sleep between the beds, out of sight. Army 'parlour games' – food for thought. Went to practise Mozart concerto in the evening and took home a couple of daffodyls for Fred which 'as personalities pleased him no end'.

Today we were on leave and had an improvised breakfast at the flat after which he went away to meet Max. It was probably a better birthday that way, I won't compete on the entertainment side any longer.

Architecture has been dropped for him this term, so we are going to have maths and statistics.

A gradual disconnection is no longer inconceivable. There is a growing realisation of the futility of wanting to completely 'own' somebody else. If he or she is in anyway worthwhile, at the best it cannot but end in a draw. If there had not been special conditions present, I should have started something long ago. As it is, I want to see more safety first. Besides, of course, there is the problem.

Coming home from the tram in the warm sun and quiet streets I was strongly reminded of Rutherglen and it was no unpleasant memory, which is rather a change and suspicious.

It seems that just having lost the taste for things without getting any new aims makes me think of the blind times as pleasant in comparison. But after all what could I get keen on?

Perhaps a mixture of work and persons which normal people will acquire automatically and which others probably can't get at all. I'm afraid it will remain extremes for me, at any rate during the war and after Fred has been out of the picture for a long time. The war can't last very long and living every day is important. The war is looking very black – maybe time to think about politics again.

Fred phoned in the evening saying sorry, would I mind etc. He's all right and going to get on once he's found his bearings. He has no exaggerated care for other people's feelings. There is an inequality which has to be constantly overcome if one cares to keep things going. Occasional slips are natural and to be expected. I've been feeling sort of dumb and unable to find words for it, all day, but it's coming to a head now – don't think anymore, don't cry any more.

THURSDAY 16 JULY

That night I went home in a shocking state after an unsuccessful book search reminding me of the old times. No clear thoughts on the matter, except considering being 'let down by Max' and feeling cheated of the day. My physical state was clearly due to psychological factors.

I forced normality for a phone call with Dr Loewe and there was a spontaneous livening up when hearing Brahms' First Symphony being whistled in one of the dark streets.

Fred came home at 5am and went on sick parade, unsuccessfully as far as evading the list, and slept most of the day, except for a 'fit of depression driving him almost crackers'. We were put on picket from 8 to 10.

That is the state of affairs I found when coming home from Essendon aerodrome, after a fairly hard but pleasant day in the country, reminding me of at least half a dozen landscapes of former times.

I offered to replace Fred from 9 on, to give him a chance to go to bed early. Observe the subtlety – not very long ago I would have made it the whole time which probably would have been unacceptable. He wanted to go to the oriental restaurant to meet Max and a girl. I thought of letting him go alone then I changed my mind; it is more comforting to face the military police being two.

Even though we did not meet any, this proved eminently wise and brought an unusual manifestation of gratitude. But we did meet two others, brothers of an artist family and well worth meeting.

The artist family to which Uwe refers is the Boyd family. Which two of the three brothers – Arthur, Guy, David – he met at this time is not known.

We came home in time. Fred was sorry to have missed the girl who turned out to be the real reason for the move rather than Max. I felt immediate relief at that, it makes all the difference and is very good news that he's even got that far. Thus, the evening was very enjoyable, a clear sky with the pale fingers of the purple search light reminding me of the war.

In the background are the newspaper headlines which have not improved but are less real. Walter keeping me company on picket just to demonstrate the other side of it. Still, comparatively speaking, I think he's better off. I've not yet learned to be prepared for these sudden changes of fortune and the constant repetition of complete happiness immediately after intense dejection.

Today I went on sick parade with a septic finger, rather reluctantly but it is advisable. It was an interesting experience though rather depressing, the whole setting smelling of distrust and hopelessness. It's easy to understand the effect it must have on people using it as a way for bludging.

FRIDAY 17 JULY

It was an unsatisfactory day. I was not able to see a minute ahead, no plans – one painful letter was all that came out of it.

In the evening Fred was at home, full of spirit. I told him to watch his wings, expecting to see them broken in the course of the evening. Amazing what 8 hours of sleep can do even though he protests that was not the reason.

We went to see Nicholson and had a very lively half hour in which Fred mentioned that he had written to Pat! No comment.

Picket 8–10. Fred was home by 12. The evening was quite good – knew what I would be doing next night!

SATURDAY 18 JULY

Next night I had dinner and drinks, two whiskeys from an American seaman, slightly drunk but still reliable with the toast – may our ships always be ready, and our ladies always be well manned. Afterwards I went to a picture with P, as described, slim and graceful, somewhat tense in his face and behaviour which is either enigmatic or just youth, the latter being far more likely at 21. The close-up was not so good. I did not think of pushing Fred into the car by pretending to remind him of something he wanted to tell Max. Home with P.H. and consequently bad temper.

P.H. may have been Peter Herbst (1919–2007), a student from Heidelberg, Germany. Uwe mentions Herbst later in the diary. Herbst, who became a celebrated philosopher, was part of the *Dunera* cohort of confirmed Anglophiles. He had lived in Britain from 1933 until his arrest and deportation in 1940. In Britain he was educated at Haileybury College.

Fred is up against terrific odds. Here bodily action seems the only thing and he won't resort to it. Still it should get him somewhat further. Today he went out again after I took his picket duty – less naturally than the first time; it does him credit that he did not like the idea at all. Of course it is O.K.

SUNDAY 19 JULY

Fred came home very late – it was 'very good and very bad'. I made a few tasteless remarks, without consequence though.

MONDAY 20 JULY

The general dissatisfaction with the way of writing these notes, which has been present for some time, became too strong to continue last night. The spirit of the moments described always evades expression and thus remains only a bare statement of facts in no way exciting as such – in fact rather bewildering, as it struck me when going to squash in the train.

I am spending all my time trying to live somebody else's life, with no success except for building up a habit which will be difficult to get rid of once it comes to that, which may be almost any day anyhow. It would be quite possible to stop it, except for the fact that there is an objective and alternative side to the matter. I think I can help a little.

I spent the evening in the quiet hut. There is a new system just to close off when I feel like it. It clears the brain completely and is time well applied as it allows me to carry on as long as I want to.

Lack of the dope, who left wordlessly before I was back from the first aid post, only accentuates the problem. He's shown some of his mettle in the Pat affair and under normal circumstances probably would have reached a higher plane by now than I will ever attain. It's a bad joke to try and advise him.

What then is left? The long-planned help in objective training, general looking after and playing piano for him, even though I always know I should be caught unprepared and inadequate in this respect. As for mental development on growing older – maybe the positions ought to be reversed. The tragedy of a life like this one is to find nothing easy or normal. I have made a very poor hand at it.

At present there seems to be increasing irritation probably forced by our continuously being together. He flew off into a rage at lunch time for no very good reasons. We were at Port Melbourne doing carpenter work all day, quite a treat for a change. Fred brightening up immediately at the sight of Stephen or Max. All this goes to prove, if I am honest enough to apply psychology against myself, that at times he must be loathing the sight of me. A natural break now may make a difference, but the light is failing and will do so even more if I am not careful.

Attachment of this sort is very much a result of the present conditions, which, on his part, seem to depend on manifestations of some spectacular sort, scramming, good squash. Yesterday he beat me more often than I him. I avoided tricky shots, but even so, it is a great improvement and should have consequences. Let's hope we can continue the training for some time. However, it's not very satisfactory in the long run. The voluntary energy will give out sooner or later and something very similar to tonight will remain. I was completely dejected and exhausted before the book on Don Quixote. There was no prospect of being mended by some miraculous changing of the other person's nature and habits. This I seem to expect, judging by my mistaking other people for Fred tonight.

As for becoming friends, this involves reaching a stable state where nothing fundamental can ever be brought into danger by either actions or words, on which further developments can only build. There is a similarity to the question of human development after the establishment of socialism. I'm afraid we are far off it.

FRIDAY 21 JULY

Further question on maths last night. There is no longer any sense in scramming together even though it would quite probably lead to similar nearness again. But what could we do together? Now his free time is sure to be employed in better ways. Cold evenings will do as far as I'm concerned and as long as we are here. There remains math and piano playing, both of which cannot be done on odd days but must be practised regularly. Still, to teach him something durable would be the next step. Don't try to influence him in human matters, probably the other way around would be more appropriate.

Last night I refrained from talking, though I woke up. This morning I only mentioned relevant matters about the book on Don Quixote and the human cavity business together with another comparison, modern lettering where no part of the character itself is represented by a line but only its shadows etc and where you see the letter nevertheless with complete clearness.

Thus, all riches were suspended in less than one hour and I was relieved to stay behind on sick parade. I spent a lazy day with indignant and useless talk to officers on the sick parade and treatment situation, and a book by T.N. Wilder, *The Bridge of San Luis Rey*.

I am looking for books, for really important books, not these one-day creations. I know far too few of them, if indeed there are many.

I found Lawrence's translation of the *Odyssey* in the evening. It is very good although I probably can't judge the full extent. It should be read together with the Greek text.

WEDNESDAY 22 JULY

Out to work again. The results of abstinence are surprising unless there are other reasons as well. Very close contact again without any action on my part except – after many hesitations because it was not all that good, nor fitting – leaving a poem by Frances Crawford on his bed last night.

Still, it did not do harm and will be the beginning of a custom, since perhaps that is the best I can do, seeing I can't give anything of my own.

It was a busy day and very enjoyable. At lunchtime in the American barracks dining room was a moment of perfect peace. Fred had gone out to buy things, but everything was at rest between us, in the state that ought to be normal. Superiority on my part with some, not excessive, interest in his affairs and none manifested in my own.

THURSDAY 23 JULY

We went out to Port Melbourne again. Stephen was cut off, reducing Fred's temper to considerably below zero, almost for the whole morning. So yesterday was not all that simple an explanation after all. At lunch we went away along the beach, out to the tip of a quay and here things changed, starting with a surprising question after a remark he had liked yesterday, about 'enjoying every look at the Royal Melbourne Hospital' which constantly gets into one's field of vision at a certain point in the camp.

I started moralising again but, thank God, was arrested right in the beginning. Then, as a link, long missing, Fred told the story of his first attachment, to somebody who, in her turn, followed a young architect. The disappointment factor from this seems to be more important than abstinence. He gave a vivid description, and I made a half serious complaint that he is always talking of himself. In fact, I owed this to him, having talked about it to Pat the night before. 'Mon amour pathetique'.

SATURDAY 25 JULY

Yesterday almost the whole group managed to come along and Fred's temper was considerably better than the day before. I did quite good work building stools. In the evening I had him and myself invited to Mrs L – Australian, journalist, pretty sharp but nice. Originally Fred did not want to come but then I asked him directly and was glad I did. With a little help his conversation was admirable, giving him a chance to reply by just seeming to think first, and he enjoyed it. For my feeling, the subjects changed too often. Unless there is some fundamental change in that after one has seen her a few times, it will soon be unsatisfactory.

The second front is more than doubtful. So, I go on living in quanta, between short lumps of sleep and always with the foreknowledge of disaster in the back of my mind. After having slept a lot this week, I came to the conclusion that it is hopeless to try and uproot the whole amount of tiredness. All I can do is to remove the top layer for which only a very short time is required. I become aware of the large quantities of fatigue left, but sleep alone cannot eliminate it. Of course, the 'other' problem still being unresolved, I should avoid all speculation.

Today Fred went for a walk, and my leave alone was quite regular. He very nicely said on leaving, 'and we shall be playing squash tomorrow'– he is improving. I remember Hausman's little poem about the changes one undergoes when being attached.

He has certain childish elements, such as bearing a grudge to a dog which soiled his coat and kicking it ¼ hour later; and blaming me for having produced his cuts on shaving, after he had showered first on my advice. These are so far difficult to understand and don't quite fit the picture of an extremely sensible and intelligent person. That he is a primate of intellect is not established or not even enough. This is the argument with Max about the necessity for maths in education, which I hope will be continued some other time without Herbst.

Fred's con spiritus face is very frequent now, so all is well. I have become quite an expert at making him talk by making some remark about him looking pleased or something of the sort and then keeping it going by short mocking remarks – it is infinitely better than merely pleading. Now that I see that it would be presumptive to attack the human end, the objective is maths and statistics. It really would do him quite a lot of good.

I made a lame attempt at letter writing. Little Susi came home earlier and there was dozing and 'watching sordid images'. I found

Little Susi was probably a fellow soldier.

Fred alone in the tent with the situation apparently the same as last Saturday, but it was a good walk and day. I called him a bloody fool for having aired his depression on Pat, particularly if he thinks of more than friendship. He fell asleep over that.

SUNDAY 26 JULY

Today he came back to that point and I'm afraid we got further into the question than I intended. It started with him suddenly declaring that he was 'going to sleep now' – which he tried and abandoned for reading. He could not avoid commenting on this behaviour, in his most graceless fashion. That broke the ice and out came the usual self-torment, especially about being unable to talk to others about anything but himself. I told him that he could be proud of himself to have got that far with all the additional handicaps superimposed on the usual pattern, which seems to apply also to Pat.

I was not convincing, I'm afraid in the end I could not really offer anything new except strongly denouncing ideas like the consultation with a psychological analyst. It would be veritable poison. The solution is successful and complete attachment. Whether it will ever come about is a question of luck, I don't think it could be forced. He mentioned his tendency to daydreaming again and the feeling of panic and oppression by being irreparably behind whenever starting studies – don't I know it!

Pat's enjoyment of little things. Sex hygiene.

MONDAY 27 JULY

I had to stop writing last night because the train was too shaky. But the cues are all that are required. I am beginning to like Pat in absence, if only for the similarity of the case and finding similar solutions without seeing the difficulties to the root.

Squash yesterday was too short, but Fred was quite good, especially with some very difficult balls. He started imitating my method of serving comfortable balls after I missed some of his crooked services, an unheard-of considerateness.

We could not get fixed up and finally went to Max's room to play records. We came back to the morning's discussion and Fred remarked that 'another thing wrong with him' was that he enjoyed being unhappy when thinking of P. In such cases my brain seems to work alright, and I came back immediately with a reproof for muddled thinking and that he enjoyed thinking of P and that he happened to be unhappy at the time. He gave me 'full marks' for that, in the identical words Ian used to employ on such occasions.

Today was nothing special except that a Philippino suddenly joined our group of three – me, Stephen and Fred – and remarked that I was the only one of us in love. He could see it in the eyes, small and lit up or something like that. We of course made fun of it but in the first moment it was a strange incident.

In the evening, I finally got hold of Mollie and arranged something for Saturday. Earlier would have been more to my taste. Rainer is leading a very strenuous night life and accordingly unpalatable, but that was my own fault too. I'm feeling guilty at having somewhat neglected him. Some time I must have a look into his state of mind.

Mary (Mollie) Turner Shaw (1906–1990), a Melbourne architect, and Helen Ogilvie (1902–1993), an artist, lived in South Yarra in a house called 'Three Little Fishes'. Mollie became friends with Uwe through her neighbour, the army chiropodist Marjorie Morris. Morris's house was called 'Ye Gods'.

Hell, things are difficult and meanwhile the sum of things is going to bits in rapid paces.

Parting from Fred is always quite enjoyable now. Yesterday at the station, today at the tram which we had to run for. There is enough attachment now, perhaps.

I came home after 12, put the laundry on his bed and said, '3 and 2 thank you'. Which made him half awake and protest against being asked for too much money in the middle of the night. 'P the bastard behaved horridly and just walked out of the library without a word'. It seems he is overdoing it, as of course he would.

TUESDAY 28 JULY

In the evening there is another case, Klaus F, a painter in a bottleneck. He is the heroic type that realises what is on and goes his own way, though of course one might ask – where? For what reason? To whose good? Which seems to be pretty good practice.

Newspaper headlines: 'Could a second front help Russia? It could mean a catastrophe!' It is now an incredible situation in England when people openly demand the 2nd front and admit at the same time that it is quite likely to be a failure. I wonder what the soldiers feel about that. I went to see Max in the rain and moonlight.

Klaus Friedeberger (1922–2019) was a former *Dunera* internee serving in the 8th Employment Company. While in the 8th he befriended the artists Sidney Nolan and Arthur Boyd, among other modernists. He continued to develop his painting style throughout the war. He went on to a successful artistic career, creating paintings characterised by keen thought and sensitivity.

Klaus Friedeberger, Sydney, 1950. The photograph was taken by Kerry Dundas. Reproduced with the permission of Julie Friedeberger.

THURSDAY 30 JULY

Busy days for a small party. In the afternoon I found a carpenter job of some sort for each person, and it was over quickly.

I went with Fred to a lecture of Plato's philosophy at the Workers' Cultural Association.

It was not very satisfactory, and the discussion was positively rotten. There was a quibble about words and questions that apparently were not in accordance with the rules of the game. There were no workers either.

Afterwards I separated to play Walter's new composition. I played it three times and have just begun to see some meaning; more required.

I met Max late, at home, after waiting outside for an hour, a rather depressing memory.

I got Mollie to talk to Fred from which it turned out that he has already passed his peak in this society, even more as far as P is concerned. 'No use for self-laceration merely to get sympathy', though of course that is putting it very crudely. Mollie thought regular work would be the thing and promised assistance. His view of things is not too convincing, too schematical, but of course one can't expect anything from somebody who knows all this world. P would be a different case but then I'm not likely to see her and am doubtful whether I should or ought to make use of an occasion of that sort. At any rate Fred ought to acquire some merit for this society by working on something.

Walking home I felt rather fed up with it all, and with seeing him in a bad temper. During the walk I forgot all about it after asking P.H. what he did with somebody else's girl he had to take out in lieu of the owner.

In the afternoon, I had told Fred a few things about his face and its dependence on his temper and promised to warn him in doubtful cases. The first time was today, but the presence of 'the group' made me superfluous and forgotten, until I became useful in the evening. Na ja.

I found that while I'm glad to know he's going to see Pat, I feel rotten when it is just one of those wasted evenings with somebody or other. This is really odd and difficult to explain, on a purely sexual basis anyway, thinking in terms of the intensity of attachment.

SUNDAY 2 AUGUST

That night I went to a philosophical lecture and fell asleep and did some other faux pas and found out in the end that I was sitting two yards away, right in the line of vision of Pat.

She was alone and we had supper together and went to the tram and missed it on account of a philosophical – anti-philosophical on my part, of course – argument and had to walk right through the city to catch another. At least she agreed to doing so. It was very enjoyable while it lasted. She is pretty and quite enthusiastic. As usual my strong arguments deserted me and only turned up afterwards. I talked a lot of rot and was glad of it afterwards when it struck me that maybe it would have been more tactful to Fred to have avoided it all. Still, meeting a human being was exciting enough and the pleasure lasted over a walk home.

MONDAY 3 AUGUST

Friday we had a good lunch walk to 'our' pier. Fred mentioned in passing that Pat had allowed herself to be manhandled on his birthday, 'more than she's likely to do again'.

In the evening I met a lumberjack at E's and got fixed up for home leave, afterwards the gliders; I could have flown the other Sunday. But there is now no longer excitement in the thought, although I should like it very much of course. No difficulty in waiting.

Saturday's appointment with Mollie was flawless. We went for a walk in the Botanical Gardens. She's all I thought and considerably more. Again, the question of getting to the case was extremely difficult. Which in Pat's case would perhaps not offer too many difficulties since we have the Dugout experiences with soldier acquaintances. She is trying to help anybody so I am a part of her war effort. We managed dinner without difficulties where I observed her taking notice of an unbuttoned tunic. On taking leave, she remarked that I should not rely on getting her again, 'not very dependable … friend who takes me out very often'.

TUESDAY 4 AUGUST

On leave and a completely improvised day but so hectic that only in the evening is there time to bring this up to date, during Loewe's lecture on gliding and Meteorology and emigrants.

After seeing Mollie home, I felt completely scattered all evening, while incidentally having to play Monopoly, of all senseless occupations. Again, I realised my own basic imperfection and incapability of ever being balanced and complete, except in short lucky moments and with considerable mental effort and alertness. I'm no good, 'a bad or painful shame', and that is about all one can say about it. Still, to draw conclusions from this state of affairs does not seem to be possible or fitting and thus I just move along aimlessly, though at times with some ease in spite of it all. Today was such a day where, for no obvious reason, everything became harmonious and pleasant. Little things bringing themselves to one's notice and letting themselves be expressed.

Sunday I answered for Fred with no compunction, so as to give him a break and long sleep. I had a lovely ride along the beach in the afternoon. In the evening we played squash better than ever before, so that even with an effort, I could not manage to be beaten more than once. Meanwhile Fred's temper grew worse and worse which was rather annoying. I told him that he was not fit to play against anybody who did not make great allowances, and that above all things, he ought to become a better loser. I did not harp on it, but the result was to be seen in today's game. I think it would have been all right even if he had been rotten and I was good. In the evening went to see the Boyd family, painter, musician; maybe very gifted but an outlet into orderly channels seems to be lacking. Anyway, they are very nice people. I played piano almost all the time, the usual pretending to have played well some time back.

FRIDAY 7 AUGUST

All the moments I enjoyed now seem drab, perhaps because I cannot remember emotions in the same way as rational things. Fred remarked when discussing the word 'luxurious' that he could not see how anyone could be too proud of his wife. When discussing friendship, P.H, quite in contrast to his usual overflowing of words, said that he knew I thought a lot of its value. I let him have it after being disdainful and cryptic in the normal way about philosophy.

I saw Pat again for a moment, but as usual only thought about it afterwards. O.K. Fred has not dropped her altogether yet.

Last night he was quite a success with Mrs L. In all it was quite a good evening, but near the end of it I felt his concentration waning and today it is at a low level. He complained about not meeting interesting people in contrast to myself which is of course too ridiculous for words. All that is wrong is that he cannot hold them, or rather neglects them after some time.

It becomes increasingly clear that we are just waiting for the one experience still missing – that its absence causes the fundamental lack of self-assertion. The present state of being incapable even of writing letters is unbearable. If it wasn't for Fred's presence…

THURSDAY 13 AUGUST

In the library – I am too tired to write anything beyond the date. Yesterday there was a strong, warm wind reminding me of flying days. I read Dutti's *Fascism*: it is mainly interesting about the role of social democracy in bringing about fascism, and even if the bad faith alleged may not have been present, there is a lot of truth in that analysis. The increased knowledge about the causes of my shortcomings doesn't alone suffice to eliminate them. There is still plenty of young boy behaviour and utterly stupid outbursts of rudeness. I'm afraid Stephen W for one is beginning to take note of the fact, not to mention Fred, who today was very bad tempered almost all the time, so that I enjoyed being separated for some time.

Suddenly there was harmony again in the evening– the mechanism is, as yet, beyond my understanding. The enjoyment of the proper working of my limbs is the only pleasure to be got out of that kind of work.

I'm rather tired of self-analysis. It has been elaborated sufficiently and now actions should be taken to bring about an improvement, if indeed it is attainable. No more poems – of others anyway. Perhaps some maths and technical work? Heaven knows how things are to go on. I wished I was in the war, really and inescapably.

FRIDAY 14 AUGUST

The news that my discharge is impending came through last night. Otherwise, I will try to get the Meteorology job, but of course that is a secondary consideration. Probably I shall regret having done so little. Still, that can't be helped now except by using what time is left. As I'm incapable of learning at present, the worry is largely illusory.

WEDNESDAY 19 AUGUST

Had a good evening at Paul's, depressing only by its evidence that I'm not sure of anything factual, only of feelings and impressions. Sunday was spent without gliding and without a girl. I had a walk in the bush of the upper Yarra Valley, regretting from time to time not being there with Mary, but with an elderly introverted man who was otherwise quite nice – again an example of how my whole thinking is being poisoned. Monday afternoon we played some tennis where I was unusually good, but had trouble with Fred, which is a more frequent occurrence these days, before there was some improvement, through the use of strong words and insistences. The enjoyment of a long, drawn backhand should appeal to him.

The mention of Mary may refer to Mary Boyd, Arthur's sister.

Afterwards we went home early, another success.

Yesterday at Bs, one of those unequal couples, in this case the man is the bully and oppressor. She is apparently not sure of herself in consequence.

Tonight everything was wrong so I went back to camp before 7 where I happened to meet K. He surprised me by asking about Fred and saying that 'Fred would never be my friend and I should be disappointed in him'. We had a long discussion which only yielded the result that he is no help either.

At work I made a fool of myself by being rude and later getting excited, and even though the meanness proposed was correct, it was unnecessary.

Fed up with all these people.

FRIDAY 21 AUGUST

Last night the news came that I am leaving this morning. I'm feeling scattered. It was a lousy day with even more than the usual amount of army red tape. Difficulties were aggravated by my incapability to be either sufficiently submissive when asking for something – or not possessed of enough personal power to cow people.

TUESDAY 25 AUGUST

Sunday I went out with the gliding club, no flying for me though. I won't spend as much energy on it as in Scotland, probably one flight would be enough for a long time.

In the evening I went to an unsatisfactory party except for a psychologist woman, who of course is difficult to get hold of. Ghastly bath.

Yesterday I was introduced to the Meteorology people and learnt that I'm going to get almost twice as much salary as I thought I would. All right if one can fill the job – otherwise the crash will be accentuated.

Looking for rooms with the usual feelings. Still hanging around – probably that is the cause of the lack of spirit. Wallowing in the 3rd movement of the first French suite, with the theme reminding me of the fugue in the double piano concerto – otherwise nothing positive on record.

I met Anita when going to some impossible place for a room. Objectively she's much nicer than I ever expected, but just as difficult to get hold of as others.

This morning I went back to camp. Nothing doing so I broke out, but ridiculous as it may seem, the mere fact that one is still tied up 'cramps our designs', just as effectively as before. Already I have little thought of Fred, but it is the one problem that wants to be solved and it remains to be seen whether any good has come of the way the last year was spent.

THURSDAY 27 AUGUST

Tuesday afternoon I was informed that my discharge had been cancelled and that I was going back to the 8th Labour Corps. It was difficult to take it seriously at first. I had a wild hope that it might be a mistake.

Concert in the evening. After that, the 'unchanging quest', which saved everything else until its unsuccessful end – and then I was too tired to think. Yesterday I spent another wasted day waiting for the transfer.

In the evening I went to see Major Layton. My first real close-up view was very unpleasant. He talked all the time, repeating himself innumerable times and was incapable of looking straight into my face. He said he was surprised at my even attempting to get out seeing the difficulties he(!) had had to get us even that far. Us having a brother in the German Army and all that. Anyway, he had no direct say in the matter, but had only been asked 'a few days ago', and expressed his opinion then, that the proper place for all three of us was the army. He advised me to drop the idea of getting the job.

I told him what I wanted to say, that I had not done anything towards getting the job, that we never thought of ourselves as Nazis and thus had no reason to complete rehabilitation when we got out. That this was the one job and that I would not stop the Meteorology Bureau people from trying to straighten things out if they so desired.

I did not enjoy Mrs Leysen's party too much after that. I'm afraid I must have not left a too favourable impression. Going back today.

Part of the company is being transferred to Albury next week, including Jobst and Rainer and Walter. What else, not to mention the general situation which is looking black enough.

SATURDAY 29 AUGUST

My first day out to work again. The other thing already very much removed from my mind, realising that Loewe probably did not mention the special nature of my case. Maybe the last chance to become normal is gone with it. But then it would have meant the end of the war which is absurd – ergo.

Everything stale and repulsive, but at times there are unreasonable clouds of cheerfulness.

MONDAY 31 AUGUST

I went out to Serkin's birthday party and got drunk, which made it a very much nicer and far longer evening than I had expected. I talked a lot of rot to some woman, quite nice and mentally substantial, but something came out of it. If we have to live again there is no sense in cutting this short, since the next may be worse than what we have got now. It may even be a case of 'it was fun while it lasted'…

Sunday was quite a good day after 2½ hours' sleep. It seems that a state of constant sleeplessness is the one most suited for this sort of life. It slows down my reactions and keeps me from dreaming and regretting. I realised that most of the disappointment at the foiled discharge was due to it having represented the end of the war for me. In reality, there is quite a good chance left for some solution of the problem.

Today was too well slept to slip into the old misery again. Fred was quite in the pink for a few days, so he was left to himself. He's made a much greater hit with the people we met, and it is only reasonable to operate separately in future. But separation altogether is not wholly to be rejected. It would do more for him.

THURSDAY 3 SEPTEMBER

Fred did not turn up Tuesday morning, in spite of advice to the contrary. It turned out that he had overslept, and he was rather apologetic about it – good. Said he would sell his soul for genius in some way, but it seems to be mainly the capability of impressing people. Eating caviar all the time – trying to escape from introversion.

I did a whole day of math and naturally finished half units. He professed an interest in analytical geometry!

I left him alone that night and went with Walter to hear Hinde, which was very good and far more satisfactory than any other march music I've heard so far, mainly on account of its clean structure.

I passed the driving test, though not nearly as safely as expected.

Wednesday, rotten work parties during the day and in the evening.

Odd moments of nobody having anything to say – but the next morning Fred was unusually cheerful and companionable. He went on night work whereas I got out via the requirement for drivers.

I left in the evening before he was in the tent, another of those changes in the earlier habits. At present there is not much energy left to feel strongly about anything. I don't think there is any other reason.

In the hall of the Australian Cinema, I saw a man whom I thought I knew – same on his part. We got talking and went up to his flat, realising that this was most likely one of the cases that would have interested Proust – and so it was.

The Australian Jewish News, 4 September 1942, p. 6.

He was fairly young, not very deep or too interesting. Another of those cases of semi neurosis gone definitely to the homosexual side. Extrovertist? He read my palm and found it 'very extraordinary', 'strong lifelines linking up with a strong love line' – which seems to be a standard method, so too the sudden 'impulsive' touch of my hand. We got talking and he must have soon realised his mistake. It may of course all be unconscious, but some of the remarks were pretty clear. He had a desire to be attractive, to be loved. As if one could help being the type that has to love himself or become like him. Or the one that attracts strong attachments. He won't see much more of me and may not try, either. When I first met him, he had been waiting for a boy who did not turn up, 'as so frequently my friends do' – I don't wonder. This shows the way I would go if I stopped being vigilant – the alternative to nihilism.

Fred was in a rather bad state after night work, too tired to sleep, suffocation complex etc. It is not as serious as it sounds since my practice of complete sympathy tends to make him forget all defence. This is a criticism of my attitude which may have to be dealt with sometime, but of course he is too highly strung to take this sort of life easy and get over it quickly. My intention to take over his night work tonight was spoiled by my getting into a night party as well. I was sorry to miss the string quartet tonight, otherwise it's all the same. Meteorology hardly exists.

The only solution for us misfits seems to be creative work. Enjoyment of moments is all right, but it cannot last without caring about my own contentment. If I could find the key to somebody else's talents, that would be the best way to help him. As for me, words will remain the only way. Purely reproducing music is bound to be inadequate.

FRIDAY 4 SEPTEMBER

Night work, and next day leave with Fred who got out via sick parade. He phoned Mollie Shaw to fix a date for us and forgot all about it and fixed one for himself at a time where he would only be able to keep it in the morning with my help. He must have felt some of my consternation but passed over it very quickly. What am I to say to that?

Tennis was not very good, too tired. Had a walk in the country with the Boyds. Mary is really very nice, though far too old for her age. Someone must have had some decisive influence there. Dog tired after so the method is not to be recommended if I want to use my time economically the next day.

Back to the Alsens – Mrs A got my first freesias after all. Susi was made up like her, her greatest ambition, which testifies to good taste besides the good character she is said to have. She will be worthwhile when grown up and let's hope luckier than her mother. Home the economical way, in the tram that doesn't go too far.

SUNDAY 6 SEPTEMBER

I went to see Mollie in the afternoon and spent time lawn mowing and making light talk. Played good squash but Fred was somewhat quiet, owing to an illusion about the score of the day before. I told him openly what I thought of it, which seemed to annoy him greatly.

Back at Mollie's for dinner. I decided to stay there for the evening and put Dr B off although I was feeling rather sorry about it when I heard that Joan was there.

Dr B is probably Dr Felix Behrend, mentioned earlier in the diary.

Mollie alluded to Fred's difficulties. We got more general about it and it turned out that she is in the same boat, which I had suspected. She had an unsuccessful love affair, 5 years to be or not to be. Architecture was started at 25 without any particular reason, 'it went click' in my head. Less creative than critical. She has an interesting collection of books, very personal, e.g. a simple Barrie, *Dear Brutus*. We arranged that she should keep Fred from talking about himself and talk shop as much as possible. Her idea for him to look for a girlfriend is probably less important. I got in a few bits about myself, but just on the 'permissible' side, I think.

When going home it struck me that probably we are both fooling ourselves, that we are not that stable or dynamic, and should feel very rotten at a moment's notice wherever the crust of habit is broken.

I found Fred in the tent chucking about his stuff and in a terrible temper. I was already half asleep when I thought better of it and got a conversation going by telling him about my faux pas with Bs, and their habit of keeping one in the dark about the attractions they had to offer on a night like that. I concealed my long stay at Mollie's place which would have demanded details. That set him right and made him talk about Daphne and the existence of strong similarities, 'introvert like myself', and physical attractions – which worry him no end, of course. I tried to persuade him to stop thinking about it, but luck is probably required to make everything work out all right. It would be tremendous…

MONDAY 7 SEPTEMBER

Today was spent driving, with a long sleep in the afternoon – on the ground.

In the evening I had a series of extremely successful phone calls. Anita happened to be in and had a very nice voice on the phone. An evening was settled, let's hope no night work will interfere. Bach and lunch with Walter – strong differences compared to Mrs A, perhaps more wrong notes, but far more musical, no Schumann or Brahms.

SUNDAY 13 SEPTEMBER

Wednesday morning it was announced that we are going to Tocumwal sometime. Moods vary between easy cheerfulness and utter dejection. Fred is to go AWL permanently – I asked him to keep me informed of his whereabouts so as to get him on to a working party list, and presented in the afternoon.

I went to a two 'man' job with A, which did not feel hard while it lasted but left me quite fagged and very much aware of T afterwards,

Members of the 8th Employment Company were stationed in Tocumwal and other places on the Victoria-New South Wales border, where they transferred goods between trains. At this time there was a break of gauge between the two states.

Men of the 8th Employment Company labouring at Tocumwal, 1945.
Bern Brent collection.

walking very slowly to Flinders Street station on a quiet red summer evening.

I went to Alsens for a complete overhaul before going to meet Anita.

When I went away from the Alsens that night I must have looked uncommonly tidy, seeing little Susi paid me a compliment. I went to Anita's without much expectation and took a single freesia along. I waited a short time outside under a verandah in the dark until Anita came and made me wait in the hall for her to put on a hat. She brought the flower back with her. She said she was very tired and had fallen asleep last night in the pictures; the same as tonight's was going to be. Asked about her job she first demanded the promise of silence in the cab, and then told me that it was work in the American Officers' Club and Hotel. Pretty long hours too – actually she ought to have been working until 10 but took it off so as not to let me come in vain.

We got out of the tram and walked along the dark street looking for the names of side streets. I knew it was further up and walked past the first while she stopped, which evoked a facetious remark about me being 'like Chinese husband' who walks three feet in front of his wife. We talked about the time in the camp, and Ottolenghi, her boyfriend, there.

The play was not very interesting in the beginning although the setting was just perfect in its smallness and intimacy. In the interval I brought things back to Ottolenghi after she had said something about the hard time she'd had in Melbourne alone and that it would be strange to have to live with her mother again.

Then she got angry and said she knew we did not like Ottolenghi, at which I protested. That he'd been uprooted and desperate and she had just helped him. Any husband would have to do a good deal to keep her. As she did not dream of marrying somebody of her class, she would have to do the living as well, so to speak. This was carried on in the next interval, 'a second drama or play'.

This light on the Ottolenghi affair showed me that I'd been an even bigger fool than I had thought, and she was much more grown up than I imagined, even then. The way she talked her Italian with him was a sign, very composed and easy. She ended by saying that they had quarrelled on the ship and not talked to each other for the first three months in the camp and that it had been a 'nice and clean affair' after that, and she was glad of the memory.

Paolo Ottolenghi (1914–1998), friend of Anita Holper, was an Italian surgeon. In 1940 he was deported from Singapore to Australia on the *Queen Mary* and interned at Tatura. The following year he left Australia for Ecuador. Later he lived in the United States, where he worked as a physician.

I got home leave the next day and had a terrible time to fix leave for Fred as well.

I remember that in the camp I once dreamed I was going to marry Anita, quite an unusual dream for me, with a feeling of fear at the responsibility, but otherwise felt content. I then talked to K about it who gravely agreed that I might do much worse than that.

It feels like one of Dunne's previous dreams, in view of that memorable day when I was told I should have to marry, on the strength of the coming splendour, and was 'picked up' by Anita in the afternoon and got the first taste of what she is really like. I had been completely justified to fall under her spell at a time when I would realise nothing of her real being. Feeling that I could talk to her about everything and need not hold back anything, in spite of the fact that we probably have little in common at present.

Just now Walter rang up to say we are meant to go to Tocumwal on Wednesday. I asked him to try and get me Anita for tomorrow or Thursday. No sense in writing letters now – I must see her.

WEDNESDAY 16 SEPTEMBER 3AM

I successfully tramped home, with the sun coming out just for the mountain part.

I rang up Anita's address and left a message saying I wanted her to ring, urgently. Waited in vain all evening and gave up hope at the end of it. A complete failure, good for going into the desert. But things turned out differently. Anita rang the Alsens in the afternoon, thus I got in touch with her. She was angry about the urgency as Walter had been ringing her the same night. It was doubtful whether she should go out with me again. 'He's mad', she told Walter. 10 minutes later was told by him that she could safely trust me.

SATURDAY 19 SEPTEMBER

I won and Anita and I spent 2 hours in a café talking in a quite new way, slow and thoughtfully, as long as important things were concerned. It drew the compliment that she liked talking to me, i.e. me talking about her. I proposed to continue in the evening.

Instead, we went dancing owing to both of us having had drinks. Mine were at Mrs L's place together with Fred, who was very dejected but got the proper treatment from somebody with whom he could not be as uninhibited as with me, had I tried.

I met Anita in the hall, but she was quite a different person, very close and familiar, which of course did not last long. In the afternoon she had looked quite strange at first, spotty. I didn't do her eyes justice; they are much better than I thought.

She has a quest for fun and a very easy manner in getting it. No wonder that people assume things from it. The body nearness is no problem here or won't be when she gets a bit older. Let's hope she'll be careful. My restraining on the first occasion turned out to be just the proper behaviour – hope there will be a change sometime, and I will try to get used to the idea of being with her.

We walked home after the dance and stood in a line for a long time talking with the man in charge – with a feeling of perpetual security and almost ancient relationship. I left her without even shaking hands and immediately afterwards got very depressed.

I had a horrid night packing up for Tocumwal. In the morning, I got out of the draft for quite ridiculous reasons while Fred had to go. I felt almost nothing, except rationally, and hardly thought of him at all during the next few days except that, if it was kismet, one could also see some advantage. KB is of the same opinion.

Fred could not have carried on in the way he did for much longer. It's doubtful whether I should reproach myself for this state of affairs. I always knew it was only for a limited period and I can't see that restraining him for the development of his character would have been any wiser, quite apart from the fact that I should feel very presumptive if I did attempt anything of the sort.

Anita had asked for a letter from me and got two so far, the first very bad, the second slightly better.

Yesterday I was forgotten by a working party and went AWL, enjoying it tremendously except for a Spenglerian depression period in the afternoon. I felt very much con spiritus and wrote to Fred about the magic of words, unfortunately lost almost altogether except for some lucky moments as that night on the *Dunera*.

I went to see the Leysens and in the first 5 minutes got into some fundamental discussion about the war and how to get over it. It was a wasted evening since I did not get hold of Anita on the phone and there were too many people.

This morning I went out with Walter and after some hesitation phoned again and was lucky! She had an amazing new voice on the phone, incredibly composed and quite deep in contrast to the high hoarse sounds across the barbed wire. She asked me to come to see her at work – whom else, I wonder? Now I'm to go to the pictures and getting more afraid every minute. But the day was lovely nonetheless.

SUNDAY 20 SEPTEMBER

We did not go to the pictures, but I met the family and we went to see some of their friends. Anita has seen all of my negligence in dress and behaviours: 'a real tramp', and I'm submitting most meekly to being educated. In the tram back, I heard that she could not read or understand my letters so the feeling that nothing important would be conveyed in that way set me right. She said quite simply it was good that I remained here and that I should come as often as I liked. She came down afterwards with the milk bottles and was very nice. Almost studious. Perhaps she is expecting it, but it remained a handshake.

Surprisingly this morning I got leave. It was glorious weather, so I dropped a letter at her house saying I wanted to go away with her for the day, with a short period of gloomy forebodings to have missed her perchance.

At Alsens I found a letter from Fred showing him in the worst possible conditions, depressed etc. It was a real horse cure of course, but I'm not yet convinced that my presence would have improved matters, quite the contrary.

WEDNESDAY 23 SEPTEMBER

Yesterday I could not bear the thought of going to work. I wanted to think it all out, so I went on sick parade with my knee and after that got into a talk with Walter, who noticed I looked depressed. I never could believe that should be so obviously written on my face but yesterday convinced me. There were all sorts of little folds which make the lot quite plain. I did not tell him much, except that I'd failed and could not go out with her any longer. He talked about a lack of routine and trying to get it going again. Nice of him. I am no longer feeling guilty with regard to Walter's schoolboy-like 'sure the physical part will be natural as soon as the mental background is cleared'. I remember the slight repulsion during the time of strong attraction, when for a moment I had the impression that she might be shallow and ordinary in some ways and not worth the effort.

I'm not really bad. My only memories from before waking up consist of half a dozen occasions when I failed or was a coward, and they hurt hellishly and have to be returned to over and over again. Now it might be different. I failed Fred occasionally, but I would not fail Anita if it came to that. The job failure in some ways was accounted for by indecision. On the other hand, it can be traced back to my own faults and thoughtlessness before the war and in the last resort to unfortunate accidents in youth – the blood poisoning at a very early age and the 'Oedipus' phenomena.

So, what is there to be sorry for as a man? I have to reckon with and overcome my faults – but at least I know their scope and have been able to extract myself from their maze sufficiently to breathe freely at least. It is typical that little importance is attached to sexual matters. At an age when one has not had the experience, one's whole thinking can be corrupted by the 'breast and mud of the soul'.

I met Walter in the evening. He had a good look at Anita last night and thought her a 'good chap' but not at all attractive, 'disinterested in that sort of thing', 'difficult nut to crack', na ja. Walter is worried about his health. I talked nicely to him and promised to find him a good doctor via Bettinger. I heard from Dr Loewe in the evening that the job is practically gone. He will make a last try tomorrow. If we don't go away I shall try to get Fred out of Tocumwal by going there myself.

Dr Hans Bettinger (1897–1975) was born in Breslau, Lower Silesia. He was appointed a pathologist at the Royal Women's Hospital in 1939.

THURSDAY 24 SEPTEMBER

For a while afterwards I felt like a cheat, seeing I did not think much about Anita for a year. But it was always there after all, just both repressed and overshadowed by another affair. Only the sexual part is missing to make it complete and worth my life. How am I to manage now, except by waiting for its fulfillment some time. There is no end to be accepted because it has not even started yet.

Some fulfillment would have been indescribably good. Now we are going to have a poor time. But perhaps she can be made to see that the static 'nice person' does not exist, that one has to make each other right.

SATURDAY 26 SEPTEMBER

I felt unable to face the way home and slept at Alsens.

It was a busy day at Sunshine, the scene of most of the days before, of heroic contemplations, fighting the Home Office, joining the Armed Forces and preparing for the time after. I had a bad time and wrote a worse letter to Fred – not posted though.

Today was quite different, seeing everything in the light of a sober early afternoon. My failure being due to procrastination, even though it is possible to construct good moral reasons for it. I was told off by Mrs Alsen for giving up the job so easily. Something is in that, and it can be seen in Anita's case too. I still have too good an opinion of myself. It will be much more exacting to live with the proper one.

I have been thinking over Tocumwal and changing places with Fred. If I want to do something special, I should fight, not give in. As it is, resignation is my strong point. I got a phone call from Rainer's girl saying he wants me to change places with him as soon as possible. So, things get taken out of my hands. What an exciting sort of life.

SUNDAY 27 SEPTEMBER

I missed the last tram and only got three hours of sleep again. This morning, leave as a Christian – I go to Albury on Tuesday.

I saw Mollie in the afternoon and Helen and a few others. She's written to Fred and suggested that he should try and draw or paint something every day and send it to her in weekly lumps – marvellous woman. Thus, for the moment, the case is out of my hands and gone into much better ones. Tomorrow I will buy paints and stuff to send along. Mollie is going to get Dostoevsky; never having read him yet. And Anita is to get the *Idiot* – I wonder, though it would be <u>the</u> book.

MONDAY 28 SEPTEMBER

Yesterday was a horrid evening at B's. I only felt alive again on the walk back when the feeling was strong that one should be together and use every minute. For some time I felt miserable at the thought that merely timidness might be at the root and then I abandoned the idea. The whole psychology complex would have been disgusting with anybody else. Even if I did not realise it clearly, the hopelessness of the present situation was always in the picture and paralysed everything. I can't seriously pretend that, thinking it over soberly, I regret it. For my sake perhaps, but not for hers. Poor foresight.

I went to bed in order to be fresh today but overslept and could have gone on for hours. I spent a successful morning. Coffee with Joan, who I'm sure could get fed up with me soon unless I pretend all the time, and lunch with Mollie. I had a lucky idea of giving her the *Kleine Blumenbuch*. After all, for the time being she is my successor for Fred. There at least I am over the hill. I am no longer blind to his faults, so it will only be friendship now, which should be better for him. He's going to go on leave by some cheating. I don't mind going away before him.

I met Layton. Pity I haven't sufficient wrath to act like a he-man and slap him in his face. I've been warned of the consequences. Na ja. While waiting for the mail corporal, the ugly type in the office asked what would become of 'my girl'. At first, I did not see what he meant and then he added, 'the very pretty tall one with black hair'.

My evening is free, thank God, I must write, and for the rest be alone. I rang Loewe and heard that the army does not want me to do the work, let alone process the discharge. So, it's over finally and nothing is left undone.

The dentist was a pleasure as usual; I really must have changed a lot. Going to B's with no particular thought in mind – apparently the approaching journey is too exciting. Vera was alone, very nice. We made a toast to having faith in the Russian meaning, and in person. She gave me a little parcel containing a sausage and a cigarette, and some freesias, yellow, blue, red – lovely.

I wrote to Anita, first wrote it in 'normal' writing and then copied it legibly. It's difficult to judge whether I ought to let her have it but I'm almost past caring. No long story asked for – 'just a piece of my mind'.

WEDNESDAY 30 SEPTEMBER

That night I walked out to St Kilda thinking lots of little scraps as in the old days. 'Passion chilled am I', feeling rather afraid of the time to come when the light fails.

After leaving the parcel, I went back to change a few words and was picked up by police who thought I was either mad or a burglar. They showed complete understanding, or at least said they did, as soon as they found out I was an Alien. A grotesque finish but not undeserved.

Noisy and tired journey to Albury. Good and quiet impression of the new place.

ALBURY, 1942

I am getting used to the new life, the first evening for a long time spent in camp. It looks as though I'm going to like it, too much perhaps. It was a lovely day, not too hot. Worked in the open which was quite bearable, with no dreary shed or station to add to the depressing sort of work. Caterpillars to be chucked about, and plenty of breaks for reading Dostoevsky's *Demon*. As usual I made a weary start, annoyed at having to get into stride, but then it was fascinating. This is the way a book ought to be written – not a minute explanation of complicated feelings and experiences that it is far more satisfactory to have for oneself, but a terse collection of facts and remarks, from which one has to get the mental position of the persons presented. It takes some capability to integrate things seen from very near, to the picture they represent from a great distance. One can't see a diamond in the x-ray view when there are only the points of the atom which glitter. Other great novelists, for example Conrad, have done it similarly and it put my mind at rest about what sort of book to write, if ever. No Proust.

Last night came back into the tent perfectly happy. Other people don't seem to disturb me any longer, especially not when they are asleep and completely inoffensive. Anita is still very real and present, even increasingly so. She has done a lot for me really. I'm feeling almost worthy and entitled to be alive, afraid of nothing and capable of everything. If I could make her forget and start all over again – but that is scarcely deserved.

SATURDAY 3 OCTOBER

Yesterday was the first rest day. I spent a morning busy with math for the first time in more than a year – enjoyable too! I've done all the things one does here. I am fed up with talking without the right partner.

What rot I write. All the old stuff long since abandoned came out of its repressed state after hitting the obstacle. Oddly enough, I feel I'm not really like that any longer. Quite a lot has changed, even if the old things are there, somewhere in the background. They can finally be eliminated at any time now, if the gods are benign. To get the courage of one's convictions is the task now. I know what I think and what is right and wrong; the thing now is to will it.

MONDAY 5 OCTOBER

That night everything went stale right down to the cigarettes, so I went to bed early after a Mozart piano concerto through the wall of the next tent. There is difficulty in writing in the tent and the danger of writing this too often. It seems the things I want to express don't lend themselves to being put down in this way. Maybe letters?

Yesterday and today were glorious days in camp. I tried 3 times to write to Mollie and nearly succeeded on the last go to get around a certain point where I drifted into self-pity, my brand, on the first two attempts. She's busy with Fred and could be no use here. Nobody could, I'm afraid.

SUNDAY 11 OCTOBER

First idea of the real Lenin pamphlet. Left wing communism to be read again and more carefully, amazing in its completeness and actuality. Long inactivity brings home the problem of this side we are fighting. What a waste of energy and time. But it cannot be otherwise, as long as everybody knows that things will have to be altered when the war is over. Even the *Times* seems to have found that out. Armed Forces versus industrial job – for personal hardening preferably. But it is not very likely to work. I felt sure I would probably die by now, but to make a proper job of living is more difficult.

FRIDAY 16 OCTOBER

Yesterday was hard work, and reading was frequently interrupted by the usual lapses into daydreams.

I spent the evening in an attempt to reply to Fred's last letter. I pointed out that 'confessions' had better be left till we meet again, then it should not be too difficult to get a step further.

MONDAY 19 OCTOBER

I went to a picture on recommendation, sceptical whether I should waste time on fictional love. Next to me sat a little boy. First there was one empty seat between us, and he wasn't sure whether he had been in that row before. Then right in the middle of the picture he suddenly said he believed that he knew me or my voice. At one time he came quite close and put his head right on my shoulder, half asleep. It felt like a girl's head with plenty of hair. Afterwards I walked out quickly to get some piano practice, in quite the mood I expected. Then suddenly the other little boy who was in the café yesterday while I was finishing the letter to Fred, came to mind. He looked at me for a moment and sat down opposite, remarking that he was hungry and going to eat. Deep blue eyes as big as the world, halting speech except when he talked of his father's revolver and tommy gun and bullets too, and how he was going to let the Japs have it. His face was far too old, with dark shadows and lines under the eyes. He had been doing work in his mother's household for 2 pounds a year. I did not pay much attention to all this at the time. As usual, I was far too cramped and bent on the petty purpose decided on before – the cursed purposefulness. When he finished, he just left, without a word.

All this came back to me on the walk under the trees and thinking about the connection with Anita. She would teach me a lot in behaving around such persons.

TUESDAY 20 OCTOBER

Got a letter from Knopf saying he is seeing Fred in a different light now and thinks they will become friends – good on him.

SATURDAY 24 OCTOBER

Don't forget to write of having advanced the Fred problem a step. For too long there was a tyrant and a slave in me. I couldn't get the friendship, yet I got the love.

I've had too much free time lately, which implies excessive smoking and getting fed up with thinking.

TUESDAY 27 OCTOBER

Perfect day, no work until lunch, letters, sun, peace. E remarked that he had never seen me looking so fit; that shows the advantages of a proper work diet, much better than having to supplement it by cross country running at nights – although the first run I had two nights ago was lovely.

FRIDAY 30 OCTOBER

Going out to work last night, I saw a surrealistic painting of multi-coloured cows in a deeply violet meadow.

Two days ago the news came that volunteers for the AIF were asked for in Melbourne. Today I learned from Jobst that according to Layton this is out of the question for us as well. I am just now beginning to grasp what it means and finding it difficult to stick to the issue, perhaps on account of the unpleasant conclusion. Making applications is as good as hopeless.

The 2nd Australian Imperial Force (AIF) comprised volunteer soldiers who served, or could serve, outside Australia and its territories. The 8th Employment Company was not part of the AIF. Wartime restrictions meant that *Dunera* men, most of whom were enemy aliens, could not serve with the AIF, though a few rare exceptions were made.

Photos of Fred – bad except one which is just bearable – momentarily make me feel uncomfortable. The photos were extremely proud and self-conscious, partly it must be a reaction to the 'gushing' of former times.

TUESDAY 3 NOVEMBER

Got drunk yesterday, didn't like it. Since Monday nothing else has happened, so a reason to be drunk. Today I saw a shockingly bad propaganda film. Plenty of army routine beforehand. On such occasions one realises the luck we have had to join a labour unit and to live here, when free time is <u>not</u> being catered for by the army people. May it last! After all, what marching we have to do is with a purpose and does not prevent one from thinking – in fact it seems to stimulate thought.

For the first time for over a year there is some purpose again.

SUNDAY 8 NOVEMBER

Horrid lazy 'half working' day and accordingly feeling down.

Neustädter's truck came rolling back in a big cloud of dust and roar from the dark shed entrance. I thought that these golden years, when one is unconscious of one's body, won't last long, unless it is because of its special working order. What a waste not to fill them up to the brim.

Helmut Neustädter (1920–2004),
later Helmut Newton, became a
famous and provocative photographer.

SUNDAY 15 NOVEMBER

Fred phoned on Friday night saying he is going on leave next week. I told him that I did not want anything except that he should enjoy himself. His reply was an emphatic 'how?' The significance of his tone only came to me afterwards. I wrote to Mollie last night indicating the situation and referring to her own idea of our first evening about what to do about it.

I read an Australian novel, *Coonardoo*. As a novel, it was nothing special, though the subject of life in the nor' west is tremendous. It's honest in giving the sex problem its due recognition and in the solutions arrived at. Sex, like hunger, when satisfied, is no trouble, or at any rate not out of proportion. Work is the thing.

MONDAY 16 NOVEMBER

Sleepy day without remorse.

I successfully kicked a football and walked all aglow to the rest hut. I am glad of the chance for a self-centred life and leisure, at any rate as long as the war lasts.

Going home on a perfect moon night, with smoke layers at the inversion over the valley. Could go on for hours.

TUESDAY 17 NOVEMBER

A lazy morning. Too much tennis in the afternoon with my service returning at last. I still have no clear idea what my future work will be.

The letter to Fred is still unwritten and that is somewhat worrying. I am feeling guilty about my inadequacy to help him to have a more enjoyable leave. That blocks the entire correspondence at present.

There is a rumour about our leaving Albury. I have no reaction, glad or otherwise, though it really is likely to be a change for the worse if it should happen.

Walter wrote. He is thinking of visiting me during his leave. I wrote warning against disappointment as regards to the scenery. One has to live here for a longer period to see the advantage of the life. I hope he'll come. The freezing of letters has left me starved for people and contact.

This morning on parade I was put on the leave list for tomorrow by mistake – a real shock, unprepared as I am. However, the real date is only three weeks off now, so it is time to get ready, make a list of books to look up, etc.

SUNDAY 22 NOVEMBER

More bits for the letter from Sidney asking for a photo of Anita's funny nose that takes its legitimate bow in one go and continues straight after that.

I almost feel like volunteering to stay here but that is a controversial issue and not far from 'bludging'.

THURSDAY 26 NOVEMBER

Events are chasing each other and it is difficult to keep pace, an ominous sign for the time in Melbourne to come next week. There is some resistance to the idea of leaving all the leisure and the beautiful surroundings, the yellow silky oaks are now in bloom. There is a chain of hills that I see from my place in the tent, with their range of colours from brown in the sunlight, to the dark blue of the last days, before tonight's 'cold wave' which made them almost disappear in the dust.

But objectively seen, Albury's role was more. It was a time of preparation for work which can be done more easily in Melbourne. Besides, too much peace is not a good idea after all. Walter's visit gave me the idea to announce my visit to Fred in another letter to reach him on return from his leave. That is all I can do, and it is probably a better idea.

Walter's visit. While sightseeing we made a stiff start with a few limits regarding topics to be discussed. We got very drunk and had a first talk about Anita. He thinks her neither pretty, nor intelligent, nor good hearted. Na ja. More important was the confession that he had talked about me. 'You deserve a better one', he said to me.

He's in a fix himself and miserable. He came to talk to 'the only person … homosexual', which I acknowledged, given the Fred affair and Anita's merit in getting me past it, if only as a 'catalysator'.

Improvising a la Vaughan Williams and ashamed of it. He mentioned that he had a commission for two arrangements and that he wanted to write a commercial symphony.

Second day with water and without alcohol. We made a slow start in the café on a subject of my own, about moving from exaggerated and unjustified individualism, via nihilism, to more social interests aiming at some worthwhile pleasures. We talked about the comparison of Dostoevsky's work and Bach, with modern novels and romantic music, where no original work is required, and one just drifts with the other's stream. He was not very interested – the old story. I want to play the organ. My own attempts showed the necessity of working out the coordination of finger movements to avoid both gaps and blurs.

Yesterday we spent the day in the camp. I read the book on Mozart which I'll try to get for him, since it happens to be relevant. It showed what I did not know, the amazing similarity in Mozart and Beethoven's lives as far as hardships go.

This evening in the hotel lounge, we drank as much drink as could be talked off in two hours. Thus, there is a method in these three days.

I was told of his wandering through various rest places and playing for people and getting them 'into a mood fit to listen to things other than the favourites they asked for'. My last suggestion was a way to create a public which otherwise doesn't seem to exist here at present. He also told of 'the other musician' who made him play variations on a theme instead of free improvisation, at the very moment when I had made the same suggestion. So, there is at last a human beginning with the prospect of development. Pity such prospects aren't open to me.

Afterwards we engaged in wild theorising about his musical development and then we went to the rest hut for a moment, and he played some really good things, variations among them, incorporating the trio themes, which he had mentioned to me before. We finished with a longish walk in the moonlight.

Albury would probably not be so good for him. Who knows whether it would be good for me in the long run? There is an opportunity for objective advancement and a start on the Bach program to be followed by Mozart, if life is long enough. For him the company of real musicians is essential and important – perhaps that is his beginning now. For the rest, he demonstrates my former symptoms being a similar case. Walter said that he knew a lot of similar cases, but they became all right in time, not being gifted with special intensity or brightness. I'm still saturated with things he has written but I have never heard; they creep into the improvising.

The visit did not help me much, but I never expected that anyway. Perhaps he enjoyed it as a whole – my personal gain being mainly the realisation of the fact that at least at last I seem to be able to give to some people and have lost some of my egocentricity. My prospects are hazy enough, but on approach they will take form. Carpentry is to be taken up again, when piano will become impractical – it can wait.

Albury is at its best on the way home to Melbourne. The faculty of appreciation was whetted but this state can't last.

MELBOURNE, 1942

FRIDAY 4 DECEMBER

I met Walter at the station. He had come from a girl, a curious creature.

If I could make a clean breast of it all, it would be to show that I am indebted for having been made a man first and then changed from a bourgeois to perhaps a revolutionary. Anita is rather young though. Albury was only the beginning. The real investigation time is to begin now, during which I might see her some time.

Longer sleep may have contributed and has to remain part of the program. It's more important than 'social evenings', of which I got another last taste at the librarian's place in Albury.

Fred phoned and praised my letters. I'm going to see him in two weeks' time, although leave does not offer the attraction I should expect. Meanwhile the labour work has assumed its proper character. No nerves about getting home late. It will be a proper proletarian education I shall get, if any.

TUESDAY 8 DECEMBER

This is Tuesday and there have been several long days with no tobacco and Russian studied only once. There have been reflections between periods of short sleep on boxes and bales, and dramatic evenings followed by impulsive notes. It is difficult to catch up with everything.

Regarding Anita, the position looks as doubtful as ever. She is too young and self-centred to be less than a full-time job. The initial inhibitions could be overcome, I'm sure, and it would be fun to find out what result our test produces in my case – but what after that? Once a start is made, I would have no choice but to break it off or go on. I sway between moments of intense longing, though somewhat impersonal, and the realisation that perhaps I ought to keep the trump card of the old burgundy for times when it can be fully appreciated and to slake my thirst on plainer stuff now. And I would be awful to live with unless some of the energy had been safely and firmly led into objective channels.

An evening at Joan's place shows the intense urge to analyse everything – a Jewish inheritance partly and the reaction of a prevented scientist.

After all, behind it there is the urge to help people – the objective, altruistic phase of growing up started with Walter. In Albury I saw a possibility to direct the analytic urge into proper channels, hence the feeling of security, superiority and, at times, conceit.

There is too much to give up. Friendship is perhaps possible for a time, during which she would at any rate see the monster properly and get a chance to show whether she is likely to catch up. There would have to be enough sexuality to suit the components of this type of friendship and perhaps some better outlet for the 'hunger' in myself; hers is as yet not due for satisfaction – if only for legal reasons. A disappointment for her would be disastrous, while I can take it.

Could one make her see all that, I wonder?

WEDNESDAY 9 DECEMBER

Today was another day of complete idleness and plenty of sleep, with the other side of this solution dominating the field. While the sexual problem has been reduced to its proper place by treating it indirectly, any success is temporary, and it remains a problem. Its solution would no doubt do me a lot of good and remove the rest of the hidden sources of depression.

Last night I went to see the Bettingers about Walter's problem.

I bought a bunch of lovely yellow flowers with some red – reminding me of the silky oak at Albury – with some compunction, since that colour belongs by rights to somebody else, and I ought to reserve flowers for her. They had huge, long stems so that holding them between my knees I had them before my eyes, in the yellow light of the tram, which even intensified their colour. Seen for moments against the cold greenish blue late evening sky, they were amazing and brought about the most perfect happiness I can so far remember – a physical burning and glowing.

The evening at Joan's place was disastrous in some ways – it shall be increasingly offensive now that there are again things I care for, unless I learn not to broadcast the fact. The night at Bettingers was an improvement. But of course, I felt so superior that it did not seem worthwhile to take the other poor mortals seriously with their affected talk about music, or even Mrs R's purely emotional and uncritical reaction. For the latter part the scientist was responsible, but the remark that escaped me, showing the illegal use made of 'light after dinner talk', may have been honest but was very unwise. I wonder if the proposed letter to Joan will make good the damage. At any rate, I'm resolved not to give her a 'piece of my mind'. Her trouble and nihilism are easily comprehensible, seeing there is no baby, no music and apparently the family adheres to economic plans. But I must wait with new experiments until the current ones show the effect of the cure, or any sign of a cure at all, since so far it is mainly analysis.

Monday night I spent 'smoko' outside, looking over the expanse of the camp, at the red sunset and the tiny new moon with occasional roars from the lions.

Melbourne Zoo is within Royal Park, which was home to Camp Pell and the 8th Employment Company. Clearly, the roars of the zoo's lions carried to camp.

Walter was in a desperate state over the news of his father's death in Poland. He felt self-reproach for not having done more to get him out in time and was in a suicidal and murderous mood, otherwise empty, griefless. We went to town together and I tried to distract him by bits of my own 'philosophy' of unimportances from the *Arandora – Dunera* origin and reincarnation. He got going and was interested in the Anita case, and later mentioned the commercial symphony he wanted to write and that one ought to call it 'Symphony Commercial on Nixonia' after the professor here who praised his more conventional works. He was the first to take my views in principle, but thought the rest was too daring 'for this country'. I was struck by this idea, but saw the full significance only hours later, in the Swedish café.

TUESDAY 15 DECEMBER

I'm on leave at last after considerable hitches and difficulties. I'm trying to clear the ground before meeting Fred again.

Thursday night I saw Mollie. Our talk was only repetitive, things thought before. However, there was at least one important new element. She mentioned her architecture research group on the problems of town planning. It started originally as a solution to a social problem, to offer assistance for a tenants' league of a slum district in the fair rents' court. A cross section through the professions shows a large body of older conservative types who dimly feel something is going on and spontaneously welcome being reproached for their insufficiency – as long as they definitely do not have to do something about it. The research group plans to bring into that sphere a considerable number of unknown architectural quantities, although the conservative layer hesitates. There is a lack of political basis in most of them and little inclination to coordinate their activities into political movements. Gradual change is preferred, with education of the masses to make them realise the necessity of new things. Mollie is afraid of metaphysics, although there is very little of it required, rather a recognition of psychology and materialistic realities, the patterns that events must follow if they are to happen at all. This recognition may be a general means of getting relief from the 'feeling of frustration' she mentioned. It appears to have been responsible for my relief at any rate.

Of course, she is right in seeing a worthwhile object in keeping the standard of a profession high when it tends to sink. Besides, action will hardly start with architecture. If the ground is prepared for ready acceptance of new ideas as soon as things in general have been changed and made them possible, that is all that could be asked for.

She will be very good then – she shows little aptitude for 'profitable' business or interest in money. She is like her eldest brother, a flying pioneer in this country, though a failure from the commercial point of view. She was never too good at horses, but after a 'rural' youth, took immediately to cars and even did some racing! She's a very good person and invaluable for me. She shows a strong similarity to Ian, in the way of momentarily closing her eyes and opening them again for the pronunciation of a vital point in an argument. If I want to meet new people, they should be those of her circle.

In a way I'm doing political work starting with Walter and now this. Also, there is the tendency to test the political reactions of workmen we meet in our jobs. Labour corps are almost ideal for my requirements, with the recent increase in time required to think about things as compared with taking in new facts. I could do with more facts but that is not under discussion at present – or any longer? It does perhaps not matter so much where I start. Thinking is the best I can do just now, and the independence and lack of responsibilities are glorious – effortless reading of papers! Thank God that at times I'm no longer my main topic.

I should be sorry if we left Melbourne just now.

I fetched Anita for the picture, being spick and span as never before. I was unjustly reproached for being for a moment inordinately proud of it. She gave a charming description of her work in a posh Bolshevik household. The pictures were very disappointing, but it was a mistake to say so as I had noticed moist eyes beside myself.

I'm afraid I enlarged on my criticism of *Mrs Miniver*, a horribly sugary and insignificant specimen of upper middle-class milieu; it may exist, but only as propaganda or an ideal! Then I talked politics again despite a few clear admonitions and my own intentions. Wasting her really. She's quite different from the scintillating face at 15 yards distance, and the more detailed beauty of the type noticed occasionally in the beginning.

But that is what she stands for at present anyway; for the rest I had better turn to Mollie Shaw. It would really be a composite ideal I am dealing with, with one component missing on the physical side.

I'm afraid Anita is now out of the race since I kissed her and was told 'you don't even know how to kiss a girl!'

I walked home at least satisfied with a manifestation of courage, though discontent for having given up too early. I wrote a letter the next evening at the Alsens, with the growing feeling of oppression and increasingly tragic notes, until I went out into the cold rainy night and found a light and more acceptable way out, laughing at the poor romantic of ten minutes ago.

Walter has been put on track by a request for lectures on fugue. In his case an objective preoccupation is the thing, pending a 'spell' I hope he will fall under sometime.

Fred's long letter is a basis for discussion. Still, he will have to find out a few brutal facts I ought to have made clear long ago. There are exciting prospects of a journey to Tocumwal.

TOCUMWAL, 1942

THURSDAY 17 DECEMBER

The journey to Tocumwal yesterday was not quite in the spirit I wanted, with some residues left over. I forgot 9d change during lunch in Shepparton and struck up an acquaintance with ACW Audrey Holmes, who pointed it out. She is a meteorologist and former art student and, so far, apparently not shocked by truth. I shall send her the Craven A cigarettes she's looking for and perhaps see her here some time.

I was met by Fred at the station, and we went for a swim in the river, after rather too many anxious comments re the snake danger. We made light talk of the things he did and friends of his friends, in the line the gang likes to talk. Flat, unattractive country and very hot, but on the whole, not as depressing as I expected. We went to town for a meal after a drunk encounter with the platoon officer and sergeant, and under difficulties got down to a real talk. Fred tends to 'shy off' into generalities and cheap intellectual concepts which are little more than a description of his troubles, and don't give much of a clue for their understanding. I found that I could not ask as directly as I wanted and then used the trick of confessing some of my experiences, without alcohol this time, which was rather more difficult. That produced at last the evidence I looked for, explaining the inability to face a problem. The old story; he was desperately in love at 16 and quite in the dark what to do about it beyond kissing. It's an explanation for the fierce hatred against his parents.

I pointed out the mental results of certain practices, if overdone. There the matter remained, as Eric came in and they got into a talk about the relative luck of being in Tocumwal instead of some other places, and what a lot one could do there.

There was not much more that night, except a remark by Fred that he had never been in closer contact with people of his own age, and that he was amazed by my interest in Camp 2. Well, that took a long time to come, but at last we are that far and there may be some progress now. I treated him differently from earlier times, frequently laughing off his tragic remarks. Perhaps he'll learn to do that himself. He has an aversion to work. That will have to be overcome by being a little less lenient with himself, and by the trick of choosing limited objectives. He could express his troubles by writing them down and telling them to me, and no one else, since I'm no longer ready to accept circulars. I told him I should expect a fundamental change in his outlook.

The talk was tending to become stale, so I brought up town planning and tried to draw him out, quite successfully for some time. I'm no longer prepared to make too many concessions. I hope the line won't break and that the fish can stand a jerk. Now it is a question of beginning at last to draw it in, while in Anita's case the line is still occasionally going out. I hope the last jerk wasn't too violent, but something must be done since it would be too late once the end of the line is reached.

MELBOURNE, 1942

SATURDAY 19 DECEMBER

Tocumwal relic – me trying to convince Fred of the superfluity of admiring all sorts of people for their knowledge or achievement. Certainly there is no reason to feel inferior, which I personally reserve for creative minds only, like artists. Anybody can reach objective achievements under the proper set of conditions, though these will condition the result or its quality to a different extent in different people.

Yesterday's afternoon passed rapidly with preparation for the 'gala evening' with Anita. To my surprise there were no hitches, neither in the gathering of clothes from all over the place, nor in keeping the appointment. She went to the theatre in an evening frock. I was rather doubtful about it at first, black and green and red, wildly mixed in stripes. Her job seems to become our permanent tram subject, but I let that go seeing there was a long evening ahead of us. She switched into Italian when I showed some evidence of grasping what she said in Russian.

The place was quite pleasant, but a little too dark for my taste. She danced somewhat too impatiently at times, getting ahead of the rhythm, getting in a few steps of her own. It's like handling a young horse, never a lull for a second, taking the lead whenever I forget to.

After the letter controversy she said uncertainly that she wished she could love me as much as vice versa.

So, I got in a quick reply, saying carefully that I was afraid the position was different now and that I was no longer in love with her, which is a blatant lie. I explained my surprise originally at finding her very much different from the usual Singapore type, but that the period of sentimental overestimation of the object had passed, that I realised now that I had been in love with what I thought her to be, rather than with the present girl Anita.

I spent the afternoon with Walter, with him still under the influence of 12 whiskeys and not quite fit for hearing all one said. He is unable to improvise other than in the commercial style. Until he writes it all down, he will repeat himself needlessly, playing and composing being analogous to talking and writing.

Jeannie supplied a valuable chapter for *Dick's Gentleman's Education* at the end of the afternoon. She made one realise that the 'accessories' of such an affair are the most difficult items to bear, the prostitution of emotions for the sake of attaining bodily satisfaction. Even pity as a motive is much better, though not much good on the whole.

THURSDAY 24 DECEMBER

I'm at the 'Blue Triangles'. Quite unexpectedly this turns out to have become a very exciting Xmas. The only present is a house, 'Little Fishes', for two days or more if I'm lucky. I saw Mollie for half an hour – just right. She wore a beautiful housecoat and there was an amazing evening sky with an unreal rainbow thrown in on the side when everything ought to have been just grey – there is something to be said for Xmas in summer.

I went to Little Fishes and had an exhausting evening. Some fencing with a Durante type of English journalist, who had rather the better of me in facts, depressing experience No.1. And

Blue Triangles, at 161 Flinders Lane, Melbourne, was a YWCA-run recreation club for servicemen and women. It offered a canteen, general lounge, reading and writing facilities, telephones and a dance room decorated with murals by Helen Ogilvie.

an attempt at talking to an economist about what I intend to do — depressing experience No.2, and rather worse than No.1. At the end of the evening I could not even utter a plain English sentence and went home under the impression that the glorious fortnight had definitely found its end, as I knew it would.

Next day was a sleepy sugar party. Most of my friends are 'mad men' like myself. These are the only people I seem to be able to associate with permanently.

FRIDAY 25 DECEMBER

I was out again, and the last café started closing and I had to go home, to camp. I got a taste of what the gods can do to one who is too sure of what things will be like. I got knocked down by a tram. Oddly enough Rainer had a rather more risky experience that day, being involved in an argument between a lorry and a tram. No third party existed in my case, and it went off easily by my giving in, with a back roll without even touching the ground with my head. Today I have the 'father of misery', the stomach, which showed what it can do. So that stopped the exultation from growing beyond bounds. Still, it is good to sit in 'Little Fishes' and have peace and long hours before me, and all regrets have since died, on account of the fine weather and the beach it suggests.

I was quite at ease at 'Three Little Fishes'. Mollie was just as usual. Later Jobst came and only recognised her after a careless remark on my part, making it into a compliment that she had changed a lot.

I was glad to sleep there another night, even though it was at the price of removing two largish spiders. Mollie can't stand them. Early morning tea at 5 and back into the army. I saw Heyward and got a list of books that look promising, maths and economics. In Germany after the war that knowledge would be a great asset.

Dick Heyward was a tutor in economics at Queen's College, University of Melbourne. From 1949 he worked at the United Nations, where he became a senior and revered figure.

This analytical way of living becomes a nuisance at times. But perhaps we all get nearer to the aims of reducing the time lag, so that experiences and digesting them happen almost simultaneously.

MELBOURNE, 1943

SATURDAY 2 JANUARY

I fetched Joan from home and pointed out my ruthlessness in applying high standards, which I explained uncharacteristically by the lack of a bourgeois background or occupation. Her contribution was limited to describing me as a 'blitz buggy'. She admitted a disinclination to give anything away of herself. Later that night at the party I saw her with her husband and felt that after all the effort he must have had to build up his relationship with her, he is entitled to the utmost consideration, even if not everything is complete or satisfactory yet.

The blitz buggy was a type of military jeep.

There was some attraction in the prospect of getting to know her well. But the friendship method would not work, only real intimacy, which no doubt would do me good. But that would demand a good deal of passion on her side, since it would be an unconventional crossing of two lines, with no 'end' in view. So, even before this talk, I doubted whether she would even consider it, in spite of the increasing phone activity. It can't be denied that things are infinitely easier for me since I need not hide or give up anything. Daphne is unconventional, but I don't feel inclined for a start – which is difficult anyway after the strategy of disinterest so far. So, at the beginning of the year there is really nothing left on that line.

I got to the party after two hours at Alsens. Mollie was very nice and natural after the long break, so the policy not to go there too often is right. Quite unexpectedly, I had the most amazing evening. That night I was remarkably un-German. In fact, a couple of German-spoken evenings that week left me very uncomfortable. These days it is only bearable in working parties.

MONDAY 4 JANUARY

Yesterday everything was preciously harmonious again until late in the evening.

I visited Knopf in the hospital and saw Walter in his new room, which was much better than I expected.

I had tea with Mollie, who often seems able to ask just the question I'm waiting for, in this case it was for the reason behind my change.

I had brought Walter some flowers; he never suspected they would be for him. I took along some of his music to 'Little Fishes' to show to a well-known Australian pianist and composer who was invited for the evening.

The identity of the pianist and composer is unknown. The orchestra leader was probably Bernard Heinze, conductor of the Melbourne Symphony Orchestra.

Besides him were the journalist couple, the man feeling badly about having, as he thought, been rude the last time. Both apparently liked me, I'm told. Also, there was a real capitalist, Baillieu of BHP fame, which was odd since I have been reading the story of their misdeeds as leading members of their firm. Also, there was the leader of the local symphony orchestra and a nice English couple. The only real talk I had was with the husband about maths and statistics. There seems to be a new army branch in need of statisticians for that purpose; if the war lasts long enough I might try that.

The general talk was extremely light. Attempts to get on to music, and from there to Walter's in particular, were foiled every time by the pianist, who was very sedate. Resting in herself, no madness, solidest background in every respect.

Finally, Mollie pushed the subject into her face, and she condescended to having a look at the music. This was before she professed strong disinclination after a bad experience with some refugee composers, whom she saw as out for an advertisement.

She read through the quartet in about 5 minutes and commented on a strong uniformity, in rhythms mainly, which I remember had intrigued me too. She seemed to be more at home reading piano music. After 10 minutes she said, 'of course it is terribly difficult to give an opinion if one has not had a good look in peace and leisure, but I don't think there is a creative spark that makes it an absolute necessity to write. Still, it is extremely workman-like, and I'd hate to close the door on anybody's efforts'.

This left me a little stunned, mainly due to the obvious inconsistency if I assume the phrase 'I don't think' to mean something more certain than 'I could not see'. I did not say anything, and it had an ungraceful finish, me having asked somewhat tactlessly whether she would not like to take the music along. Mainly for Mollie's sake I was able to make up for that before she left, while the consternation was as strong as ever.

When the others had left, I voiced my doubts and found strong opposition. Finally, we agreed to explain it as a misunderstanding of the words used, although Mollie maintained that in architecture, for example, she could be sure of detecting a 'spark' immediately. My point was that it would be very difficult anywhere, and particularly in music. I learned of the pianist's preference for Brahms amongst better composers.

By now I have come to a different view, that I approached the whole undertaking with the wrong attitude. All I could have done was to get the reaction of somebody competent, never to expect or ask for a 'verdict' which must be doubted whatever way it falls, unless I am deeply convinced of the judging person's competence and know her well. I must explain this to Mollie and ask her to repair the damage, if any.

This morning Walter took it coolly and, interestingly enough, discovered the inconsistency at once, although if anything I took great pains to give a description coloured the other way.

Even if she is right, it would not amount to as much as I felt yesterday. The way his mind works when composing, the insistent nature of his ideas which can't be placated by substitutes, makes me feel still that she is wrong, but of course I'm extremely likely to be biased here. Apart from the objective opinion on his work, which is probably obtainable only by waiting for a long time, the more subjective aspect, as 'making order of the chaos in one's own mind', is perhaps far more important and one should forget the 'immediate reward'.

At any rate, this event began the decline I had been expecting since the afternoon, when everything seemed perfect in the frame of the 'delicate, or Melbourne' period. And in consequence, perhaps to forcibly restore the balance, I fell to talk to Mollie on the Anita issue again, without being able to convince Mollie that she is wrong in considering myself 'four times as valuable as that girl', and in expecting that 'I shall be hurt.'

I talked of the decline I am now used to after each peak, which led us to her own troubles. There is a deep dissatisfaction somewhere, usually coming to a head when staying among familiar surroundings, that reminds her of a hard time with her family. There is an unsuccessful attachment; both of them wanted to give but neither wanted to accept. She interrupted with a nihilistic comment by describing it as ridiculous and fantastic, but cleansed of these controlled emotions, there is a distinct picture of unhappiness in what she said. My very first impression was right enough, even if the conclusion – 'no good for me' – became outdated. She said I was a tonic by taking her attention away from herself.

I went home very late, wondering about it all and whether I could help her. In some ways our needs seem to be perfectly suited, but the matter is bristling with difficulties and that solution may not be what she needs. It may go much too far but I should probably get over anything that can possibly come of it.

Before I saw Mollie on Friday night, I had a foreboding of being told one of these days that we had better end it all, and of accepting it completely unmoved, and going away in a state of emptiness. But then, Mollie in her warnings thinks of other things, those that would maybe happen if there was a 'happy end'.

Today the day passed rapidly with heavy coffee bags with plenty of sleep in between.

There is a similarity between the 'components' – Mollie and Anita – forcing themselves to be happy, to accept realities that can't be changed and naturally losing control at times. Walter's impression that Mollie does not think too highly of Anita is quite sound. Her attraction to working class people was a shrewd point to mention last night. Mollie could do such a lot for her. The trouble is that again I could not define Anita's interests; perhaps life away from the family will let them come out more clearly.

WEDNESDAY 6 JANUARY

Yesterday's plan of doing some work at the college – at least as much as I'm able after a couple of essential letters to Fred, setting out a few points relevant for the task of enjoying life – was foiled when I went to Little Fishes and only got through the letters very late. I had a short conversation with Mollie who had been attempting to write to me, apologising for her gloomy comments on Sunday night, for talking of herself. She even had thought of suggesting that henceforth I should avoid the place. Not much was said on either side. The extreme contact was gone, which is probably as it should be. The intended promotion to more than the rational part of what I'm looking for can't be maintained and would endanger, has already endangered, the whole.

It is interesting to see her inability to accept Anita. It's either envy or class prejudice. She shows a difficulty to take any other than the intellectual approach.

THURSDAY 7 JANUARY

This morning news came that Fred's crowd is coming back tonight, which made it a bearable day in spite of the sugar party. I rang Mollie and after giving her the news, blurted out something about the 'disgusting character of the factory'. Now I'm afraid she is going to send along some investigator, which may be somewhat too strong a measure after all. It is a general trouble. My imagination is always assisted by plenty of unused energy to give things more emphasis than they appear to deserve soon afterwards.

SUNDAY 10 JANUARY

Three days ago news came that the Tocumwal detachment would return in the evening. Before going to the station, I went to see Walter. I found him asleep and altogether reluctant to wake up. But that had advantages since he said exactly what he thought: 'started on Mollie yet? – she would make a man of you'. I have pondered over this additional evidence ever since. Of course, the subject is now on the cards.

Fred made a good show at the station and a pretty bad one in camp and the next day, when they were treated very much the same way as we were on our return to the bosom of the company. Still, it takes some time to find the ground under one's feet again and there definitely has been some improvement. His reactions are devoid of humour and show an extraordinary lack of proportion. But there is some sense for humanity beyond the limited crowd he is used to, and with a little will, effort and some luck he might do quite well. Going through town with him is an effort now. My newly acquired sense of guessing the right thing to do and at the same time having in mind one or two alternatives, fails me. But as a rule, we won't go out together now.

Now it is Sunday afternoon and soon I shall have to go back to camp to take Fred's place at fire guard duty. For once this way of thinking does not seem to work and I had just better record the remaining facts.

I got a lift from a man in civil clothes who makes a habit of picking up soldiers to tell them that he was in Malaya and wounded, so as to reassure himself. There was a comic note when he asked where I came from and after some hesitation, very short though, I said: 'Germany'. We shook hands and he said I was the first man he had met who had the guts to admit such a fact, and he then enlarged on the subject. He was slightly, very slightly, tipsy, I suppose, still the compliment was made quite consciously. He talked of the inability of people here, living as we do, to realise the fact of war and consequently to 'cut out' petty complaining.

Then I went to Little Fishes and had a nice evening except for the last few remarks, where I mentioned the lack of cooperation from Anita regarding the concert. Mollie quickly reverted to her warning, which made me feel ashamed seeing that she must now have quite the wrong impression of what the trouble is. I meant to ask her to take an interest in Anita, for her own sake and not as a help for me.

However, that takes some nerve now and is not fair on Mollie.

I went back to camp feeling 'stuck in the climb'; my brain is evidently overdrawn. I should get some other food, since there is emptiness on listening. Only after some time, a few weak notes. I realise that I must not expect help from anybody else, as Mollie said in defending her decision not to invite Fred yesterday, but to invite me, as I'm capable of dealing with myself. It remains to be found out whether the once missing experiences should be forced or, whether on the contrary, it would be a bad thing to have a break down in my convictions.

SATURDAY 16 JANUARY

H came in last night with some peaches. I always feel oddly young in his presence although he is only a couple of years older. He's a reticent type who probably finds it difficult to be in close contact with people, and with me it's easy, under the circumstances.

With a solid job in hand I could live with Anita. On the other hand, I can see what the psychological consequences would be; a gradual return to self-centredness. But a miserable existence would not suit the other part, or not yet anyway. She might reach sufficient detachment – but should I be glad about that if it happened?

Uwe Radok, circa 1940s.
Radok family collection.

SUNDAY 17 JANUARY

We went to the pictures. The wild west pictures came on first, with some tough fights. I looked out for excitement but there was none visible. In the interval before the Great Dictator came on, I made a remark that I might have chosen another program had I known that this was possibly the last time I should take her to the pictures.

Then came the picture. An odd mixture of comic-tragic real scenes of the war and the Nazi time – which so far I can't wholly appreciate from an artistic point of view, as an intrinsic part of the whole, and as necessary contrasts – and superb scenes of the dictator personality.

It was almost the real thing, the caricature touch being so subtle as to be forgotten frequently by the onlooker. Very clever ridiculing of his speech technique – long unintelligible passages as they would almost sound to an English audience, translated into one English sentence of 3 or 4 words – and later the typist making a whole sheet of a single syllable and, vice versa, the dictator nodding assent.

Afterwards we went into a crowded café and sat opposite two nasty looking, slightly drunk civilians. Not the atmosphere to keep going perhaps, or had there been too much of it already that evening? I confessed to exhaustion and there was only small talk. I noticed a packet of red Capstan cigarettes and a box of matches, which were not there any longer when a girl came to the table and said she had left them by mistake. I expected that the fellows would hand them over at once, but they didn't.

Under the circumstances my indignation was too slow in rising and I only got out a belated biting remark which passed unnoticed. I could see the possibility of a fight and said to Anita that I wouldn't take that course with her present.

Though it 'didn't matter', there was discord and not much was said in the tram back or on the final walk. I took to staring into the void, but being asked for my thoughts could only say that they were bits and pieces and used an earlier one, about the difficulty of saying 'nice things' at will. I realise now that nicety must not be my own to make it bearable.

She was quite unaffected by my gloom and sang and talked all the way home. In the tram there was a short interlude when I got a characterisation of some passengers, and comments on the peaceful face of a sleeping baby. In fact, her observational gift and knowledge of people is an invaluable contribution for me who, in order to get my department into working order, had to live behind double doors and carpeted walls in seclusion for a long time, and incidentally may never be qualified for a specialised job on account of that.

I went away in a daze and felt gloomy immediately afterwards, realising that it was what I saw as cowardice in the cigarette encounter that had spoiled the rest of the evening for me. Waiting for the night tram in the rain, my thoughts came into order.

No heroic feat was required or even suitable. There was only a failure in not seeing at once the way of settling the case satisfactorily for all my standards – to suggest that the bloke had put them into his pockets by mistake. This probably would have appealed to his good nature, if any, and opened a decent way out for him.

This morning I was in almost too good a mood – poor Fred was feeling very low and having to listen to unusual chatter. Before going to Little Fishes, I went to H's room and had some good music and I found some more amazing books/coincidences in the library – *Mourning Becomes Electra*, Browning poems.

WEDNESDAY 20 JANUARY

I went to Queen's College and enjoyed aloneness walking into the quadrangle in bright moonlight.

THURSDAY 21 JANUARY

Yesterday I was part of a horrid working party in the morning. It was quite enjoyable in the afternoon, when the beginnings of a headache were made to disappear immediately by the willed drugging of work.

I went out with Mollie and saw a bad picture. It serves me right since I forgot that there must be no artificial, fiction life now, besides the one I am lucky enough to have at my own disposal. It is difficult to concentrate on any other person just now. It took all evening to get into tune and only outdated talk came of it. The plan was to have Anita at Little Fishes more often, to give her the same experience I enjoyed there – intellectual contacts of great diversity open to one who is not yet committed, owing to circumstances. But then, her interests are not yet or may never be in persons on the intellectual side. Some of one's own intellectual life is required first, which makes it profitable to me to see persons through her eyes, even if it leads nowhere in particular. This idea was another anticipation.

On the strength of a few 'married moments' Mollie made me a compliment of having an innate curiosity, and stressed the spinster psychology in *Wuthering Heights*, the tendency to wallow in one's emotions and the incapability of seeing anything valuable beyond them. This is relevant and I ought to concentrate more on the facts, the way we lean towards each other in the doorway, than on the reflections next day which require far more condensation and are secondary compared to the actual play.

Today I had an argument with a nasty fellow, and a string of invectives nearly brought me to fighting pitch although I knew it was not worthwhile. It was my own fault. Anyway, why do I bother about such people, 'save it for a great victory'. Living beyond my legitimate means offers a sufficient number of 'prickly pears'. I needn't take on everyone that comes my way. Nietzsche again.

The dope may have become too habitual. If only its good constituents could be preserved there could be a way out.

In all, this was a good, single constructive evening. It wound up with a discussion with H, enjoyable as usual since we always agree, either on the conclusion or on the difference that prevents our arguments being identical.

TUESDAY 26 JANUARY

Anita and I were waiting for the tram. I was tired. Getting out of the tram my arm was not right, 'too hard', meaning plenty of muscles – 'oh you are just a sissy' (!) to which boasting of strength was no adequate reply. But this was unexpected and forebode an end when talks no longer last for an evening. The window in her flat was still lighted and it made her immediately restless. She slipped away with 'thank you very much'. I should have forced her back for a moment.

I planned this record for Sunday but unfortunately did not get to it. Instead, I spent a single-minded morning at 'Little Fishes' and Walter's place. In spite of qualms, I rang Anita to ask whether she'd care to come to the beach with us. I decided on looking in before we went out, even though she had said, 'if I can have the place to myself, I'd rather stay here'.

Then things got badly out of hand. In reply to the sissy enquiry, I was told that she meant all it could mean. There was a half apology immediately afterwards, 'I seem to tread on everybody's foot today'.

In the end, we all went out together, which I had not intended. We left the tram on an impulse and walked to some shabby park along the shore. There was a triangular talk, and I was incapable of control, so I just watched the dam break, with Walter applying a few good pushes. 'He's too good for you', then she said, 'I can't make him out – always restless (thinking), never at ease, letting himself go to do what he wants or likes, German' etc.

At last Walter went, after trying to arrange a party at his place. 'Now he will start preaching' – that is Fred's one-time complaint too! – 'but I shall just run away'.

FRIDAY 12 FEBRUARY

For once I will copy the letter I sent to Anita here, as it is written just as much to myself as to her.

> Anita
>
> This is my first and last real letter to you. Forget about the plan of meeting my friend Mollie, it was not meant to be an effort but only possible as a generous gift – and you have not been at peace for long enough that you could afford to be generous again.
>
> You were mistaken when you thought (as you told Walter) that I should not understand your wish not to see me anymore. Very often when I came to you I was prepared for being told just that – for I knew all the time that you are too good for me in my present state. I think of you as of a precious and exquisite vase which once a fool touched with his clumsy hands, starting vibrations of an intensity in its thin glass walls that may in the end destroy it.
>
> I myself, another fool, thought I could make these vibrations come to rest, and for a time I seemed to succeed. But I was clumsy too and only added some small vibrations of my own instead. These will die away soon and at least I did not leave you worse off than I found you. I'm glad of that and my failure can't touch any longer what came before. For a few moments I saw you in all your manifold loveliness – your face which is sometimes quite empty and then suddenly lit up by your thoughts, sometimes resting like the 'voluptuoso' sea and there again showing an intensity of life I never dream of. Or your voice changing quickly from the tinny flatness of an Australian to the deeper rich notes of the Russian. What does it matter now that I am blamed for robbing you of your peace when you told me at such a moment that I had been 'best of the lot'? For the first time in my life I felt completely at peace and I'm grateful for that and for what I saw.

Keep this sheet anyway; you will be able to remember what you were like. And if you don't care, somebody else may – the person you deserve for having been born lucky or in a single cast without rift. Somebody who will listen to you when you want to be heard (as I did) and who will take you away from mad talk if you can't find out of it yourself (as I did not) and who will show you a way for putting to good use your intellect of a man (as I might have done, had I been less of a fool).

Don't think too badly of the fool though he is not altogether responsible for his defects. I was made a 'sissy' by bad luck and spent all my life fighting against it. Always taking on things too big for myself. First there were nightmares – and when I had got rid of them I thought I had to learn flying; can you imagine what it feels like to be, as a boy of 15, thousands of feet up in the air alone with nobody on earth to help if anything goes wrong, as often happened?

Again, now I think that I ought to help making a better world, as my last ambition. Perhaps I can't help remaining a coward in some small personal matters when I feel obliged to take on jobs that require ready courage.

But for you I would have to be courageous by nature and that is why I think you are right in telling me to quit. So I shall not see you anymore – unless you ask for me. Don't consider that altogether impossible! You have been a comet to me which I saw as a faint light from afar and lost sight of again; which then crossed the path of my dark star unexpectedly. I knew then there would follow another encounter, according to the laws of comets, before you would go back into space. But comets also sometimes return if they are not caught up by a bigger star in the meantime – or scattered into debris that appears as shooting stars and still reminds of the former splendour. So you might return – find me strong enough to hold you then – or cold and dead, which would not be the worst solution and would save myself and others a lot of troubles and disappointments.

You have gone very fast and far during the last few days – talking to you was no good since you could no longer see what I meant. That is why I preferred to write – even though you may not even read to the end of the letter. I wish you the happiness you want, and I shall always be glad to see you and ready to help you if I can, and be prepared to see you leave again, as one who has been 'married for a long time' sometimes must be' (do you remember that phrase of yours?). I won't move any nearer on my own accord and you shall have all the peace you want from me.

Yours

R

These are my thoughts after reading through most of the last two years' notes, finding them surprising at times, but exhausting as a whole and no longer topical. Except that they show the stages very clearly, and that Anita was kept in mind all the time.

They are unintelligible at times, discussing things thought relevant in the book, the job conceived on too large a scale. Understanding is what is wanted. Actions need to follow conditions and be bound to material necessity as realised at an earlier time. There need be no fear of chasing after a soap bubble. Whether concrete realisation of this fact would be solid enough a foundation to justify living with somebody else may still be doubted.

The objective after all is marriage. Obstacles are no job or security or means on my part, no independence of surroundings or peace on hers. So we've got to wait and improve separately. A formal agreement would have no reality practically. Trust in fate and the laws of comets. She's not the proper person yet altogether, but more completely than anyone before her.

EPILOGUE

Uwe continued the diaries until mid-1943, when he stopped abruptly. This coincided with news that his Scottish friend Ian Brown had died in a plane crash. Ian's mother sent Uwe a note saying that Ian had loved Uwe and left him his bible.

In 1944 Uwe started working at the University of Melbourne in the Meteorology Department. In May that year he married Anita Holper, mentioned in the diaries. Their first daughter, Claudia, was born the following March, Helen in November 1947, and Jacquie in May 1957.

Radok family collection.

In 1966 Uwe succeeded Fritz Loewe as Reader in Charge of the Department of Meteorology at the University of Melbourne. Uwe established an internationally respected research program, particularly in Antarctic glaciology, forging links with the Bureau of Meteorology, the CSIRO, the Snowy Mountains Hydro-Electric Authority, and the Weapons Research Establishment. With collaborators, Uwe pioneered numerical weather prediction in Australia, and made globally important discoveries on the mechanisms of clear air turbulence. He spent the last years of his career in Boulder, Colorado, before retiring to Australia. Radok Lake in the Prince Charles Mountains in Antarctica was named in his honour.

A 1968 profile of him by a colleague noted that he aroused and maintained interest as much by letter-writing as by rapid conversation and pungent comment. He was famous for his sartorial splendour while on field excursions. His style, best described as 'international war surplus', featured an irregular camouflage design.

This photograph of Uwe was taken in the 1980s. Helmut Newton, whom Uwe knew during their internment at Tatura, is believed to have been the photographer.
Radok family collection.

Uwe died in 2009, aged 93. He remained friends with Fred and Walter all his life. Anita died in 2014, aged 89.

Uwe had pre-emptively penned his own obituary in 1999, noting that he had an unusual and outstanding ability to bring scientists together, and in demonstrating and being praised for generosity in giving credit to younger scientists and colleagues in cooperative projects, even when he was responsible for the ideas and much of the work. He specified that no funeral or memorial should be held for him.

His ashes were poured into the sea from the trawl deck of the *Aurora Australis* as it sailed alongside a 30-mile iceberg to the north-east of Davis Station in Antarctica. The day was windy and misty with wind lanes of crushed ice from a nearby iceberg, a little over a kilometre away. There were snow petrels and Antarctic fulmars in the air and on nearby ice floes. A large adult orca was sighted swimming alongside the ship during the brief and informal ceremony.

Snow petrel.

Uwe had kept his diaries safe in a tin. In 2007 he passed them on to his daughters, perhaps assuming his cryptic handwriting would make them indecipherable. Jacquie used the opportunity of a COVID lockdown in 2020 to transcribe them. As she worked through 12 diaries containing 120,000 words, she discovered a side of her father that his family had never known.

ACKNOWLEDGEMENTS

Our thanks to Kate Garrett for her thoughtful translations, Cressi Downing and Helen Spark for expert editing and proofreading, and Christina Twomey, who was an early and enthusiastic supporter of this project in her role as Head of the School of Philosophical, Historical and International Studies at Monash University. We extend a double thanks to Christina for co-writing the introduction. As always, Carol Bunyan gave prompt and wise advice. She is an exceptional scholar and a generous one.

For help on points of detail and much else, we thank Mary-Clare Adam, Bern Brent, Kathy Buchanan, Pam Buchdahl and family, Martin Burman, Claire Dobbin, Claudia Downing, Malcolm Downing, Tonia Eckfeld, Daniel Fabian, Julie Friedeberger, Susannah Helman, Anne Holloway, Mark McKenna, Andrew McNamara, Kate Nancarrow, Eleni Papavasileiou, Stephanie Radok, Uwe Radok (son of Christoph), Kara Rasmanis, Margot Schreiber, Sabine Schreiber, James Skvarch, the Stocky family, Joseph Toltz, Mark Topp, the Wurzburger family, and archivists at the Wiener Library, London.

The team at Monash University Publishing is a delight to work with. Thanks to Greg Bain, Sarah Cannon, Julia Carlomagno, Jo Mullins, Les Thomas and Sam van der Plank.

Wayne Houlden, Rhiannon Tanner and Helen Spark were ever encouraging and patient. To them, above all, our thanks.

INDEX

THE EDITORS

Jacquie Houlden is Uwe Radok's daughter. She is an author, educator and business woman. During Covid lockdowns she opened a tin containing her father's wartime diaries and began transcribing them, uncovering a surprising story.

Seumas Spark is an Adjunct Fellow in History at Monash University. He is a co-author of *Dunera Lives: Profiles* and *Dunera Lives: A Visual History*, and co-editor of *'I Wonder': The Life and Work of Ken Inglis*.

THE TRANSLATOR

Kate Garrett holds a Master of Translation Studies from Monash University. She has a particular interest in the translation of historical documents, poetry and memoirs related to the Second World War.